Magdalen College
Oxford
Feb. 11ᵗʰ 1945

My dear Sarah — Please excuse me for not writing to you before to wish you a merry Christmas and a happy New Year and to thank you for your nice Card which I liked very much; I think you have improved in drawing cats and these were very good, much better than I can do. I can only draw a cat from the back view like this . I think it is rather cheating, don't you? because it does not show the face which is the difficult part to do. It is a funny thing that faces of people are easier to do than

most animals' faces except perhaps elephants and owls . I wonder why that should be! The reason I have not written before is that we have had a dreadfully busy time with people being ill in the house and visitors and pipes getting frozen in the frost. All the same I liked the frost (did you?); the woods looked really lovely with all the while on the trees, just like a picture to a story. But perhaps you were in London. I suppose it was not so nice there. We now have a Baby, about 6 weeks old, living in the house. It is a very quiet one and does not keep any of us

C. S. Lewis
Letters to Children

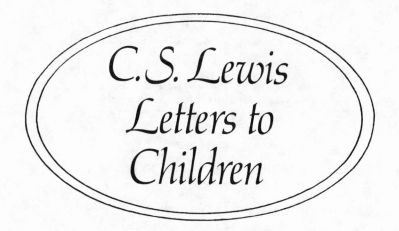

C.S. Lewis
Letters to
Children

Edited by Lyle W. Dorsett and
Marjorie Lamp Mead

FOREWORD BY DOUGLAS H. GRESHAM

COLLIER BOOKS

MACMILLAN PUBLISHING COMPANY

NEW YORK

Foreword © 1985 by Douglas H. Gresham
Letters © 1985 by C. S. Lewis PTE Limited
Notes, Introduction © 1985 by Lyle W. Dorsett
and Marjorie E. Mead

Collier Books
Macmillan Publishing Company
866 Third Avenue, New York, NY 10022
Collier Macmillan Canada, Inc.

Library of Congress Cataloging-in-Publication Data

Lewis, C. S. (Clive Staples), 1898–1963.
C. S. Lewis letters to children.

Bibliography: p.
Summary: A collection of letters from the English author of the
Narnia books to a variety of children.
1. Lewis, C. S. (Clive Staples), 1898–1963—Correspondence.
2. Lewis, C. S. (Clive Staples), 1898–1963. Chronicles of Narnia.
3. Authors, English—20th century—Correspondence.
4. Children—Correspondence.   5. Children's stories—
Authorship. [1. Lewis, C. S. (Clive Staples), 1898–1963—
Correspondence.   2. Authors, English—Correspondence]
I. Dorsett, Lyle W.   II. Mead, Marjorie Lamp.   III. Title.
IV. Title: CS Lewis letters to children.
PR6023.E926Z48   1988   828'.91409   [B]   88-9545
ISBN 0-02-031741-7

Macmillan books are available at special discounts for bulk
purchases for sales promotions, premiums, fund-raising, or
educational use. Special editions or book excerpts can also be
created to specification. For details, contact:

Special Sales Director
Macmillan Publishing Company
866 Third Avenue
New York, NY 10022

First Collier Edition 1988

10   9   8   7   6   5   4   3   2   1

Printed in the United States of America

Letters to Children is also available in a hardcover edition from
Macmillan Publishing Company.

To Ryan Wayne Mead

Contents

Foreword

DOUGLAS H. GRESHAM

I FIRST MET C. S. Lewis late in the year 1953. I was only eight years old then but I can still remember our meeting. My mother said "Jack, this is Doug; Doug, this is Jack," like grown-ups always do, and we shook hands. Jack was his nickname, you see, and all his friends called him that. His real name was Clive Staples Lewis; I think Jack was nicer.

From the very first, Jack and I were friends. He showed my brother and me all around Oxford, where we climbed right to the top of the famous Magdalen Tower, up a dark narrow spiral staircase that seemed to go on forever until at last we came to a short ladder, and then out into the bright sunlight high above the roofs of Oxford. We could see for miles. In 1956 Jack and my mother were married and I went to live at "The Kilns"; this was the name of Jack's home. Many houses in England have names, and this one was in the middle of eight acres of garden with woods and a lake.

Jack was the exact opposite of all the "stepmothers" in the fairy tales; he was kind, jolly, and generous. He bought a pony for us, and when I got interested in canoes, he bought me a kayak. He even let me paddle him across the lake in it. We explored the woods together and went for walks. Sometimes Jack would give me some pages of things he was writing and ask if I liked them. I usually did, but if I didn't, he was the kind of man who would listen to what I said.

After my mother died, when I was fourteen years old, Jack and I became very close. You see, mother loved Jack and mother loved me, so for Jack and me a little bit of her lived on in both of us. One of my strongest memories of Jack was the evening after my mother died. It was the first time I ever saw a grown man cry. He put his arm around me, and I put mine around him, and we tried to comfort each other.

Jack too is gone now, but he lives on for me in my memory, and for all the world in his writings, and for you in this book.

It's fun laying out all my books as a cathedral. Personally I'd make *Miracles* and the other "treatises" the cathedral school: my children's stories are the real side-chapels, each with its own little altar.

C. S. LEWIS (Unpublished letter to Professor WILLIAM KINTER, March 28, 1953)

Introduction

FORTUNATELY FOR THE MAIL CARRIER at Headington Quarry near Oxford, England, not everyone on the route was as famous as C. S. Lewis. Daily for over twenty years, except holidays, stacks of cards and letters were delivered to The Kilns, Mr. Lewis's red brick home. As regularly as the mail arrived, the professor sat down at his desk and answered the correspondents. Indeed, nearly every morning he spent an hour or more reading the mail and writing out replies.

C. S. Lewis was prominent because he wrote fascinating books. His volumes of fairy tales, science fiction, Christian theology, and literary criticism were devoured by people all over the world, especially in Great Britain and America. Many of his readers wrote to ask questions or to thank him for his books; others inquired when the next volume would be published, while some simply described what the books meant to them.

Lewis received mail from individuals as diverse as the books he wrote. Correspondence came from all kinds of people: famous and obscure, young and old. Although answering so many letters could be tedious, he responded personally to each one, often writing in longhand with a dip-pen and ink. Sometimes the inveterate writer was assisted in this task by his brother Warren, who—after his retirement from the Royal Army Service Corps—served as Lewis's secretary and typist.

Among the many letters Lewis received were thousands of fan letters from his young readers of *The Chronicles of Narnia*. The author believed that answering these letters was a God-given duty, and his replies reflect the concern and care that he brought to the task. He once described it this way: "The child as reader is neither to be patronised nor idolised: we talk to him as man to man. . . . We must of course try to do [children] no harm: we may, under the Omnipotence, sometimes dare to hope that we may do them good. But only such good as involves treating them with respect. . . . Once in a hotel dining-room I said, rather too loudly, 'I loathe prunes.' 'So do I,' came an unexpected six-year-old voice from another table. Sympathy was instantaneous. Neither of us thought it funny. We both knew that prunes are far too nasty to be funny. That is the proper meeting between man and child as independent personalities."[1]

Lewis's own direct contact with children was limited. Although his American wife, Joy Davidman, provided the long-time bachelor with an instant family, Lewis's marriage came far past middle age; indeed, his two stepsons, David and Douglas, were half-grown when they moved into The Kilns. And even then, the boys spent too many months away at boarding school to teach Lewis much about children. Furthermore, the professor wrote his children's books before he ever met Douglas and David, even though some of the volumes were not published until later.

In fact, Lewis's understanding of children came from another source: it came from within himself. The same year in which he finished the last of his Narnian stories Lewis wrote: "When I was ten, I read fairy tales in secret and would have been ashamed if I had been found doing so. Now that I am fifty I read them openly. When I became a man I put away childish things, including the fear of childishness and the desire to be very grown up."[2]

Most of the letters in this book were first sent to Lewis because the young correspondents had read one or more of the Narnian tales. (There is, in fact, only one exception to this rule—the letters from Sarah, his goddaughter.) Many of these children continued to write Lewis about a variety of matters as their pen relationship deepened, but the majority of their questions still centered on the Narnian books, the spiritual reality within these stories, and the craft of writing itself. Not surprisingly, these were the same topics Lewis was often asked to address by his adult readers.

When Lewis began to write *The Lion, the Witch and the Wardrobe*, his vivid imagination—his love for dressed animals, knights in armour, and all things faerie—pulled him inevitably in the direction of fantasy. The actual writing began with an image. As Lewis explained: "I see pictures. . . . I have no idea whether this is the usual way of writing stories, still less whether it is the best. It is the only one I know:

images always come first."[3] Making the point another way, he mentioned that "Some people seem to think I began by asking myself how I could say something about Christianity to children. . . . I couldn't write in that way at all. Everything began with images; a faun carrying an umbrella, a queen on a sledge, a magnificent lion. At first there wasn't even anything Christian about them; that element pushed in of its own accord."[4]

As Lewis was writing the first of his Narnian tales, he was certainly aware that Christianity had begun to slip quietly into his story. But it was only after reflection that he began to see "how stories of this kind could steal past a certain inhibition which had paralysed much of my own religion in childhood. Why did one find it so hard to feel as one was told one ought to feel about the sufferings of Christ? I thought the chief reason was that one was told one ought to. An obligation to feel can freeze feelings. . . . But supposing that by casting all these things into an imaginary world, stripping them of their stained-glass and Sunday School associations, one could make them for the first time appear in their real potency? Could one not thus steal past those watchful dragons? I thought one could."[5]

These concerns that filled Lewis's mind when he wrote his children's books were evident when he answered his letters from children. A kind man, he was never more compassionate than when he wrote to young people. He remembered well the fears, questions, and joys of childhood, and he understood his young correspondents. Lewis met them on "common, universally human, ground"[6] and they responded. The editors hope that you too will find in these letters "common ground."

❖

Because these letters were written to children, a short sketch of C. S. Lewis's childhood follows this introduction. The letters themselves are arranged chronologically, using only the first names of the recipients. No attempt has been made to collect and print all of Lewis's letters to children. The number is too large and the author frequently repeated himself. What we have selected is a representative sample. Deletions in the text were made only to promote clarity and remove redundancy; the editors' additions are indicated by brackets: [   ]. Originals or photocopies of the letters in this book are housed in either the Marion E. Wade Collection, Wheaton College, Illinois, or the Bodleian Library, Oxford. An annotated bibliography of books and related items of interest to readers of Narnia completes the text.

The editors thank Evelyn Brace, Ruth J. Cording, P. Allen Hargis, and Brenda Phillips of the Marion E. Wade Collection for their assistance. We are also grateful to Douglas H. Gresham of Tasmania, Australia, for his friendship and support. Finally, we are indebted to Alexia Dorszynski, our editor at Macmillan, for her vision and good judgment.

C. S. Lewis: His Childhood

CLIVE STAPLES LEWIS was born on November 29, 1898, in Belfast, Northern Ireland. His father, Albert, was a lawyer, and his mother, Flora, a mathematician and the daughter of a minister. He had one brother, Warren, three years older, who was to become his closest friend.

Writing in his diary when he was eight years old, C. S. Lewis described his family this way: "Papy is of course the master of the house, and a man in whom you can see strong Lewis features, bad temper, very sensible, nice wen not in a temper. Mamy is like most middle aged ladys, stout, brown hair, spectaciles, kniting her cheif industry. I am like most boys of 8 and I am like Papy, bad temper, thick lips, thin, and generaly wearing a jersey. . . . Hoora! Warnie comes home this morning. I am lying in bed waiting for him and thinking about him, and before I know where I am I hear his boots pounding on the stairs, he comes into the room, we shake hands and begin to talk. . . ."[1]

The two brothers' chief delight each year was their summer seaside holiday. First came the serious business of selecting which toys to take, the flurry of activity as they were packed, and then the thrill of a horse-and-buggy ride to the train station. The train ride itself was climaxed when they arrived at their glorious destination—the sea!

Because their father hated being away from the routine of his work and the security of his home, the boys traveled alone with their mother and their nurse, Lizzie. In her letters home, Flora would keep her husband informed of their sons' activities. When young Clive was not yet two years old, his mother wrote (using one of his many nicknames of Baby, Babbins, Babsie, and Babs): "Babsie is talking like anything. He astonished me this morning; Warren sniffled and he turned round and said 'Warnie wipe nose'. . . . He asks for you often, and thinks that men he sees passing in grey coats are Papy. . . . He is quite reconciled to the piano. . . ."[2]

A year later his mother again wrote to Albert from their seaside holiday: "Yesterday was a dreadful day, poured and blew all day, such wind I never heard in my life before. . . . As I had to go out I bought the children two little boats with men in them; we made paper fishes, and Baby spent most of the day making his man catch fish by the primitive method of jumping over the side and bringing the fish back with him. . . . The place suits Babs well. . . . He has made great friends with the Station Master; he went up with me today to get the papers, and as soon as he saw him in the distance he called out, 'Hullo Station Master'. The station is being painted now, so you will understand how attractive it is to the children. . . ."[3]

A few days later Flora continued: "Here is a little story of Babbins to amuse the old people. I took him into a shop to buy a penny engine and the woman asked him if she should tie a string to it for him. Baby just looked at her with great contempt and said, 'Baby doesn't see any string on the engines that Baby sees in the station'. You never saw a woman so taken aback. He is just infatuated with the trains; no matter where he is, if he sees a 'siglan' down he has to be taken back to the station. . . ."[4]

Before Clive Staples Lewis was four years old, "he made the momentous decision to change his name—disliking that of Clive and no doubt feeling it beneath the dignity of his years to continue to be addressed as Babbins or Babs. Anyway, one morning he marched up to [his] mother, put a forefinger on his chest, and announced 'He is Jacksie'; an announcement no doubt received by [his] mother with an absentminded, 'Yes dear'. But on the following day he was still Jacksie, and as he refused absolutely to answer to any other name, Jacksie it had to be."[5] In fact, so determined was young "Jack" that even his parents accepted his new name, and so he was to be known as Jack Lewis by his family and friends for the rest of his life.

Jack's principal playmate as he was growing up was his brother, Warren. Together they rode bicycles, played board games such as chess and "Snakes and Ladders," watched trains and boats, painted pictures, wrote stories, went swimming, cared for pets, and read books. In most ways, their lives were remarkably like the lives of children today—with one major exception: when it rained, which it did often in Belfast, the Lewis brothers were not allowed outside.

This rain-time restriction was the result of the

danger of tuberculosis, a disease dreadfully more serious in the early 1900s than it is now. Keeping children warm and dry was a parent's best defense
against the threat. Warren later described this regula-
tion: "Playing in the garden was by no means an
every day affair, for the weather ruled our lives to an
extent which must seem incredible [today]. . . . To be
caught out in a shower without an overcoat was a
minor disaster which entailed changing all your
clothes the minute you got back to the house; on
threatening days you were allowed to use the garden,
but only on the strict understanding that you came
indoors on the first spot of rain; and on wet days it
was forbidden to leave the house under any pretext
whatever."[6]

These long, rainy days became a source of abid-
ing pleasure for Jack and Warnie. If they grew bored
with their toys they took up drawing. Warren painted
steamships; Jack drew "dressed animals." Little by little an imaginary country began to emerge, and soon
Jack was writing his first stories, the adventures and
history of Boxen. (These tales were not published in
his lifetime, but they suggested the way the grown-
up Jack would later write his stories of Narnia.)

In 1905 the Lewis family moved to a new home,
Little Lea, which delighted Jack and Warnie. Here in
the suburbs of Belfast, the boys were able to explore
"real country," as they phrased it. For the first time in
their lives, a brief bicycle ride brought them to the
beauty of the open, hilly Irish farm country. This delight in the rural land of their childhood remained
with both brothers throughout their lives.

Jack and Warren had more than the open land to

survey; there were the vast recesses of Little Lea to explore. Warren described their new home as "perhaps the worst designed house I ever saw, [and] . . . for that very reason a child's delight. On the top floor, cupboard like doors opened into huge, dark, wasted spaces under the roof, tunnel-like passages through which children could crawl, connecting space with space; and every now and then one would discover a rectangular pit, floored with the ceiling of a bedroom; space which the architect had despaired of putting to any use. Best of all, we had 'our' attic. In the old house our joint bedroom had also been our day nursery, but now, with a day room 'of our very own', never tidied by officious maids, Boxen and all that it stood for entered upon its golden age."[7] Jack was later to use some of these same memories in the creation of Polly and Digory's attic play area in *The Magician's Nephew*.

Little Lea held other treasures as well. There was a seemingly endless array of books: "books in the study, books in the drawing room, books in the cloakroom, books (two deep) in the great bookcase on the landing, books in a bedroom, books piled high as [a child's] shoulder in the cistern attic, books of all kinds . . ., books readable and unreadable, books suitable for a child and books most emphatically not."[8] Among these bound volumes the Lewis brothers frequently wandered, emerging with some new book to occupy a long rainy afternoon.

Another of their rainy-day occupations was described years later by a cousin, Claire (Lewis) Clapperton. In Little Lea there stood a tall, dark oak wardrobe which had been hand-carved and assembled by their grandfather. The children would climb into the wardrobe, sitting quietly in the dark, "while Jacks told us his tales of adventure."[9] This same wardrobe later became the inspiration for the doorway into the land of Narnia.*

In May 1905 the pattern of the boys' life changed when ten-year-old Warnie was sent away to boarding school in England. Though this was the usual practice in upper-middle-class British homes, leaving home at such a young age was nonetheless difficult for both children and parents. In Warren's case the circumstances were made worse by the intolerable conditions of Wynyard School where he was sent. Run by a mentally unstable headmaster, the boys in his care were given little instruction, their days filled largely with boredom and fear. Warren understandably hated Wynyard and asked to be brought home. His parents, though concerned by his unhappiness, were unaware of the school's real abuses and chose to keep him enrolled.

In contrast, Jack's life at this time continued to be happy as his letters to Warnie at Wynyard show: "My Dear Warnie," he wrote in November 1905, "Peter [a pet mouse] has had two un-fortunat adventures since I last wrote, how-ever they came out all right in the end. Maud [the housemaid] was in her room, and heard Peter howling. When she came down, what do you think? Sitting on the floor ready to spring on Peter was a big BLACK CAT. Maud chased it for a long way. I was not able to help matters because I was

---

*This wardrobe has been preserved as part of the Marion E. Wade Collection, Wheaton College, Wheaton, Illinois.

out on my bych. . . . On halow-een we had great fun
and had fireworks, rockets, catterine wheels, squbes,
and a kind of thing you lit and twirled and then they
made STARS. We hung up an apple and bit at it,
we got Grandfather down to watch and he tried to
bite . . ."[10]

Jack and Warnie's imaginary country, Boxen,
continued to be an important part of their friendship
and it remained so for the rest of their lives: "My dear
Warnie, I am sorry that I did not write to you before.
At present Boxen is SLIGHTLY (?) convulsed. The
news has just reached us that King Bunny is a pris-
oner. The colonists (who are of course the war party)
are in a bad way; they dare scarcely leave their houses
because of the mobs. In Tararo the Prussians and
Boxonians are at fearful odds against each other and
the natives. Such was the state of affairs recently: but
the able General Quicksteppe is taking steps to res-
cue King Bunny. (The news somewhat pacified the
rioters). yours loving brother Jacks."[11]

Early in 1908 Jack first learned that his mother
was critically ill. "It was in fact cancer and followed
the usual course; an operation (they operated in the
patient's house in those days), an apparent convales-
cence, a return of the disease, increasing pain, and
death."[12] On August 23, 1908, after a long and pain-
filled illness, Flora Lewis died at Little Lea. Jack was
nine, and Warren, thirteen. Years later Jack wrote,
that with her death, "all settled happiness, all that
was tranquil and reliable, disappeared from my
life."[13]

His mother's death, plus the passing of a grandfather and uncle the same year, shrouded Jack in an

atmosphere of darkness that lingered for years. During this difficult time the boys' father, although a loving man, offered little consolation. A man seldom given to enthusiasm for anything but his work, he was now more downcast than ever. Both boys suffered from their father's mood, and the sadness they felt was increased by their removal to boarding school a few weeks later.

As difficult as these years were, something positive came from it all. Decades later Jack drew upon the memory of his mother's illness when writing *The Magician's Nephew*. In this book Digory's mother nearly suffered the same fate as Flora, but Aslan intervened before it was too late.

Although providential intervention did not prevent Jack's mother's death, life did improve for him by 1914. That year he went to Great Bookham, Surrey, England, to study with a private tutor named Professor W. T. Kirkpatrick. Nicknamed Kirk and The Great Knock, this brilliant gentleman inspired and trained Jack Lewis by challenging him and pushing him to his limits. Kirkpatrick's program for young Lewis was just what the teenager needed. Indeed, forty years later Jack was to look back at his days in Great Bookham and write: "If I could please myself I would always live as I lived there. . . . My debt to [Kirk] is very great, my reverence to this day undiminished."[14] This debt of gratitude would be repaid in part through the naming of Professor Digory Kirke in the Narnian books for his well-loved tutor.

In December 1916, after two full years with Kirk, Jack received a scholarship to University College, Oxford. After several years of study, interrupted by service in World War I, the brilliant scholar commenced a career of over forty years of writing and teaching—a vocation that lasted until his death on November 22, 1963.

NOTES

Introduction

[1]C. S. Lewis, "On Three Ways of Writing for Children," in *On Stories and Other Essays on Literature*, ed. Walter Hooper (New York: Harcourt Brace Jovanovich, 1982), p. 42.

[2]Ibid., p. 34.

[3]Ibid., p. 41.

[4]C. S. Lewis, "Sometimes Fairy Stories May Say Best What's to Be Said," in *On Stories and Other Essays on Literature*, ed. Walter Hooper (New York: Harcourt Brace Jovanovich, 1982), p. 46.

[5]Ibid., p. 47.

[6]C. S. Lewis, "On Juvenile Taste," in *On Stories and Other Essays on Literature*, ed. Walter Hooper (New York: Harcourt Brace Jovanovich, 1982), p. 51.

C. S. Lewis: His Childhood

[1]W. H. Lewis, *C. S. Lewis: A Biography*, p. 16. (Unpublished biography in the Marion E. Wade Collection, Wheaton College, Illinois).

[2]Ibid., p. 6.

[3]Ibid., p. 7.

[4]Ibid.

[5]Ibid., p. 8.

[6]Ibid., p. 3.

[7]Ibid., pp. 13–14.

[8]C. S. Lewis, *Surprised by Joy: The Shape of My Early Life* (New York: Harcourt, Brace & World, 1956), p. 10.

[9]Unpublished letter to Clyde S. Kilby from Claire Lewis Clapperton, August 20, 1979.

[10]W. H. Lewis, *C. S. Lewis: A Biography*, pp. 12–13.

[11]Ibid., p. 14.

[12]C. S. Lewis, *Surprised by Joy*, p. 18.

[13]Ibid., p. 21.

[14]Ibid., pp. 141, 148.

A Note to Children

WE HOPE that you enjoy these letters. They were written to children just like you who read and loved *The Chronicles of Narnia*. C. S. Lewis said that he wrote these tales because they were the sort of books he "would have liked to [have] read when [he] was a child." And though the letters in this book do not have your name on them, consider that they are yours. For surely, if he could have, C. S. Lewis would have written them to you.

The Letters

[C. S. Lewis, a professor of English Language and Literature at Magdalen College, Oxford University, had published fifteen books by the time he wrote this letter in 1944. Although he carried on an extensive correspondence with his adult readers, he seldom wrote to children until the first of his Narnian books, *The Lion, the Witch and the Wardrobe*, appeared in 1950. One of the exceptions to this was his godchild, Sarah. The daughter of a former pupil, Sarah lived in a small town south of London. This letter was written during World War II when certain foods in Great Britain were scarce.]

❖

July 16th. 1944

My dear Sarah—Thank you very much for sending me the pictures of the Fairy King and Queen at tea (or is it breakfast?) in their palace and all the cats (what a lot of cats they have! And a separate table for them. How sensible!). I liked them very much. It must be nice for them (I mean the King and Queen) having so many currants in their cake. We don't get many now, do we? I am getting to be quite friends with an old Rabbit who lives in the Wood at Magdalen [College]. I pick leaves off the trees for him because he can't reach up to the branches and he eats them out of my hand. One day he stood up on his hind legs and put his front paws against me, he was so greedy. I wrote this about it;

A funny old man had a habit
of giving a leaf to a rabbit.
At first it was shy
But then, by and by,
It got rude and would stand up to grab it.

But it's a very nice Rabbit all the same; I call him "Baron Biscuit." Please tell Mummie I thank her for her nice letter. I didn't have a bad time in the Home but they didn't give me enough to eat and they washed me all over as if I wasn't old enough to wash myself. Have you ever met a hospital-nurse? They are very strong-minded women. No more now because I am still not quite better. Lots of love to you and everyone else

> your affectionate godfather
> C. S. Lewis

❖

> Magdalen College
> Oxford
> Feb[ruary] 11th. 1945

My dear Sarah—Please excuse me for not writing to you before to wish you a merry Christmas and a happy New Year and to thank you for your nice card which I liked very much; I think you have improved in drawing cats and these were very good, much better than I can do. I can only draw a cat from the back view like this . I think it is rather cheating, don't you? because it does not show the face which is the difficult part to do. It is a funny thing that faces of people are easier to do than most animals' faces except perhaps elephants and owls . I wonder why that should be! The reason I have not written before is that we have had a dreadfully busy time with people being ill in the house and visitors and pipes getting frozen in the frost. All the same I like the frost (did you?): the woods looked really lovely with all the white on the trees, just like a picture to a story. But perhaps you were in London. I suppose it was not so nice there. We now have a Baby, about 6 weeks old, living in the house.[1] It is a very quiet one and does not keep any of us awake at night. It is a boy. We still have our old big dog, he is eight years old. I think this is as much for a dog as 56 is for a man—you find this out by finding what is seven times the dog's age. So he is getting rather grey and very slow and stately. He is great friends with the two cats, but if he sees a strange cat in the garden he goes for it at once. He seems to know at once whether it is a stranger or one of our own cats even if it is a long way off and looks just like one of them. His name is Bruce. The two cats are called "Kitty-Koo" and "Pushkin". Kitty-Koo is old and black and very timid and gentle but Pushkin is gray and young and rather fierce. She does not know how to velvet her paws. She is not very nice to the old cat. I wonder how you are all getting on? Are you at school now and how do you like it? It must be about half way through term by now, I should think. Do you keep a "calendar" and cross off the days till the end of term? I am not going to post this till tomorrow

---

[1]During the war, children were often evacuated from London to the country to protect them from German air raids. The Lewis household took in many of these evacuees. Lewis later began *The Lion, the Witch and the Wardrobe* with evacuation of the Pevensie children from London to Professor Kirke's country home.

because I want to put in a "book-token". You take it to a book-shop and they give you a book instead of it. This is for a kind of Christmas present, only it is very late. Now I have written you a letter you must write me one—that is, if you like writing letters but not otherwise. I used to like it once but I don't much now because I have so many to write, but my Brother does some of them for me on his typewriter which is a great help. Have you seen any snow-drops yet this year? I saw some two days ago. Give my love to the others—and to yourself

Your affectionate god-father
C. S. Lewis

[The following letter to Sarah on her confirmation included a cover letter to her mother:]

[3 April 1949]
As from Magdalen

Dear Mrs. N . . .

The enclosed is a desperate attempt to do what I am v.[ery] ill qualified for. After writing it it occurred to me that I might have said all the things that you (knowing Sarah) might know to be particularly disastrous. So I thought you'd better vet it before passing it on. I'm so clumsy.

Blessings on all three—and I'm sorry I can't come. But I'd only have behaved like an ass if I had!

Yours ever
C. S. Lewis

[3 April 1949]

My dear Sarah

I am sorry to say that I don't think I shall be able to be at your confirmation on Saturday. For most men Saturday afternoon is a free time, but I have an invalid old lady[2] to look after and the week-end is the time when I have no freedom at all, and have to try to be Nurse, Kennel-Maid, Wood-cutter, Butler, House-maid and Secretary all in one. I had hoped that if the old lady were a little better than usual and if all the other people in the house were in good tempers I might be able to get away next Saturday. But the old lady is a good deal worse than usual and most of the people in the house are in bad tempers. So I must "stick to the ship".

If I *had* come and we had met, I am afraid you might have found me very shy and dull. (By the way, always remember that old people can be quite as shy with young people as young people can be with old. This explains what must seem to you the idiotic way in which so many grown-ups talk to you). But I will try to do what I can by a letter. I think of myself as having to be two people for you. (1) The real, serious, Christian godfather (2) The fairy godfather. As re-gards (2) I enclose a bit of the only kind of magic (a very dull kind) which I can work. Your mother will know how to deal with the spell. I think it will mean one or two, or even five, pounds for you *now*, to get

---

[2]This lady was Janie King Moore, the mother of C. S. Lewis's army friend, E. F. C. "Paddy" Moore. When Paddy was killed in World War I, Lewis honored his promise to care for his friend's mother and sister, Maureen. Mrs. Moore died in 1951.

things you want, and the rest in the Bank for future use. As I say, it is a dull kind of magic and a really good godfather (of type 2) would do something much more interesting: but it is the best an old bachelor can think of, and it is with my love.

As for No 1, the serious Christian godfather, I feel very unfit for the work—just as you, I dare say, may feel very unfit for being confirmed and for receiving the Holy Communion. But then an angel would not be really fit and we must all do the best we can. So I suppose I must try to give you advice. And the bit of advice that comes into my head is this; don't expect (I mean, don't *count on* and don't *demand*) that when you are confirmed, or when you make your first Communion, you will have all the *feelings* you would like to have. You may, of course: but also you may not. But don't worry if you don't get them. They aren't what matter. The things that are happening to you are quite real things whether you feel as you w[oul]d. wish or not, just as a meal will do a hungry person good even if he has a cold in the head which will rather spoil the taste. Our Lord will give us right feelings if He wishes—and then we must say Thank you. If He doesn't, then we must say to ourselves (and Him) that He knows us best. This, by the way, is one of the very few subjects on which I feel I do know something. For years after I had become a regular communicant I can't tell you how dull my feelings were and how my attention wandered at the most important moments. It is only in the last year or two that things have begun to come right—which just shows how important it is to keep on doing what you are told.

Oh—I'd nearly forgotten—I have *one* other piece of advice. Remember that there are only three kinds of things anyone need ever do. (1) Things we *ought* to do (2) Things we've *got* to do (3) Things we *like* doing. I say this because some people seem to spend so much of their time doing things for none of the three reasons, things like reading books they don't like because other people read them. Things you ought to do are things like doing one's school work or being nice to people. Things one has got to do are things like dressing and undressing, or household shopping. Things one likes doing—but of course I don't know what *you* like. Perhaps you'll write and tell me one day.

Of course I always mention you in my prayers and will most especially on Saturday. Do the same for me

Your affectionate godfather
C. S. Lewis

❖

Magdalen College
Oxford
[9 January 1950]

My Dear Sarah

Yes, I did indeed get the mats and was only waiting to be sure of the right address before acknowledging them. They were so like lino-cuts that if I weren't such an unhandy and messy person I w[oul]d. have been tempted to ink them and try making a few prints. Thanks very much indeed. I'm glad you like the Ballet lessons. I'm just back from a weekend at Malvern and found an awful pile of letters waiting me, so I am scribbling in haste. But I must just tell you what I saw in a field—one young pig cross the field with a great big bundle of hay in its mouth and deliberately lay it down at the feet of an old pig. I could hardly believe my eyes. I'm sorry to say the old pig didn't take the slightest notice. Perhaps *it* couldn't believe *its* eyes either. Love to yourself and all.

> Your affectionate
> godfather
> C. S. Lewis

❖

> Magdalen College,
> Oxford.
> 26th. January 1951

My dear Sarah,

I am 100% with you about Rider Haggard.[3] You know he wrote a sequel to *She* told by Holly, and called *Ayesha*; *She and Alan*, told by A. Quartermain: and *Wisdom's Daughter* told by She herself. What comes out from reading all four is that She was (as Job assumed) a dreadful liar. A. Quartermain was the only man who wasn't taken in by her. *She* is the best story of the four, though not the best written. A mis-

---

[3]Sir Henry Rider Haggard (1856–1925), English novelist and fantasy writer.

sionary told me that he had seen a little ruined Kraal where the natives told him a white witch used to live who *was* called She-who-must-be-obeyed. Rider Haggard had no doubt heard this too, and that is the kernel of the story.

I also have just had 'flu or I'd write more. Love to all.

> Your affectionate Godfather,
> C. S. Lewis

❖

> Magdalen College
> Oxford
> 22nd. January 1952

Dear [Carol],

It is a pleasure to answer your question. I found the name in the notes to Lane's *Arabian Nights*:[4] it is the Turkish for Lion. I pronounce it Ass-lan myself. And of course I meant the Lion of Judah. I am so glad you liked [*The Lion, the Witch and the Wardrobe*]. I hope you will like the sequel (*Prince Caspian*) which came out in November.

> Yours sincerely,
> C. S. Lewis

[4]Edward William Lane (1801–1876), translator of *The Thousand and One Nights*, better known as *Arabian Nights*.

[26 January 1953]

[To Sarah:]
Thanks for most interesting letter and congratulations on the good time you seem to be having. Just as you are going back to old experiences in liking parties again, so I am by pulling out one of my teeth with fingers the other day, wh.[ich] I can't have done for many a year!* I liked *Mrs. Masham's Repose* far the best of White's books myself.[5] Our Christmas was conditioned by having a visitor for nearly 3 weeks: a very nice one but one can't feel quite free.[6] Love to all

Yours
C. S. Lewis

*This is the beginning of Act V, I suppose?

❖

[21 March 1953]

Dear Michael

I see I have thanked your Father for a kind present which really came from *you*. Let me now say Thank *you*, very much indeed. I think it was wonderful of you. At least I know that when I was a boy, though I liked lots of authors, I never sent them any-

[5] T. H. White (1906–1964), Englisn fantasy writer. *Mistress Masham's Repose* is a story about a little girl and a community of "Lilliputians."

[6] This visitor was Joy Davidman Gresham, an American friend and correspondent, who was later to become C. S. Lewis's wife. While visiting England, Joy was invited to spend Christmas 1952 at The Kilns as the houseguest of Lewis and his brother, Warren.

thing. The reason there is so much boiled food here is, of course, that we have so little cooking-fat for roasting or frying.

The new book is *The Silver* CHAIR, not CHAIN. Don't look forward to it too much or you are sure to be disappointed. With 100,000 thanks and lots of love.

yours
C. S. Lewis

❖

[One of C. S. Lewis's early fan letters on *The Chronicles of Narnia* came from the United States. Hila was eleven years old when she wrote this letter, complete with a water-color painting that she had done of all of the characters in *The Lion, the Witch and the Wardrobe*. Her first reading of this story was three years earlier when she experienced what she described years later as "an indefinable stirring and longing."

At the time this letter was written, *The Lion, the Witch and the Wardrobe* (1950), *Prince Caspian* (1951), and *The Voyage of the "Dawn Treader"* (1952) were the only books published; *The Silver Chair* would appear later in 1953. However, Lewis had actually finished writing all of the seven volumes a year earlier, in 1952.]

June 3rd. 1953

Dear [Hila]

Thank you so much for your lovely letter and pictures. I realised at once that the coloured one was not a particular scene but a sort of line-up like what you would have at the very end if it was a play instead of stories. The [*Voyage of the*] *"Dawn Treader"* is *not* to be the last: There are to be 4 more, 7 in all. Didn't you notice that Aslan said nothing about Eustace not going back? I thought the best of your pictures was the one of Mr. Tumnus at the bottom of the letter. As to Aslan's other name, well I want you to guess. Has there never been anyone in *this* world who (1.) Arrived at the same time as Father Christmas. (2.) Said he was the son of the Great Emperor. (3.) Gave himself up for someone else's fault to be jeered at and killed by wicked people. (4.) Came to life again. (5.) Is sometimes spoken of as a Lamb (see the end of the Dawn Treader). Don't you really know His name in this world. Think it over and let me know your answer!

Reepicheep in your coloured picture has just the right perky, cheeky expression. I love real mice. There are lots in my rooms in College but I have never set a trap. When I sit up late working they poke their heads out from behind the curtains just as if they were saying, "Hi! Time for *you* to go to bed. We want to come out and play."

> All good wishes,
> yours ever
> C. S. Lewis

❖

[23 June 1953]

Dear Hila

(I never met this name before. What language?) You have got it right. No: the three stories you know are the only three that have yet come out. The fourth will be out this Fall (as you say: we say "this Autumn"). I am so glad your friends like the books. It's funny they all began with the second one. All good wishes,

yours
C. S. Lewis

❖

14th. Sept[ember] 1953

Dear Phyllida

Although your letter was written a month ago I only got it to-day, for I have been away in Donegal [Republic of Ireland] (which is glorious). Thanks v.[ery] much: it is so interesting to hear exactly what people do like and don't like, which is just what grown-up readers never really tell.

Now about *kids*. I also hate the word. But if you mean the place in *P.[rince] Caspian* chap 8, the point is that Edmund hated it too. He was using the rottenest word just because it *was* the rottenest word, running himself down as much as possible, because he was making a fool of the Dwarf—as you might say "of course I can only *strum*" when you really knew you could play the piano quite as well as the other person. But if I have used *kids* anywhere else (I hope I haven't) then I'm sorry: you are quite right in objecting to it. And you are also right about the party turned into stone in the woods. I thought people would take it for granted that Aslan would put it all right. But I see now I should have said so.

By the way, do you think the Dark Island is *too* frightening for small children? Did it give your brother the horrors? I was nervous about that, but I left it in because I thought one can never be sure what will or will not frighten people.

There are to be 7 Narnian stories altogether. I am sorry they are so dear: it is the publisher, not me, who fixes the price. Here is the new one [*The Silver Chair*].

As I say, I think *you* are right about the other points but I feel sure *I'm* right to make them grow up in Narnia. Of course they will grow up in this world too. You'll see. You see, I don't think age matters so much as people think. Parts of me are still 12 and I think other parts were already 50 when I was 12: so I don't feel it v.[ery] odd that they grow up in Narnia while they are children in England.

yours sincerely
C. S. Lewis

❖

[19 September 1953]

Dear Phyllida

I feel as one does when *after* "showing up" one's work one realises one has made the very same mistake one got into a row for last week! I mean, *after* sending off the book, I read it myself and found "kids" again twice. I really will take care not to do it again. The earlier part of Rilian's story, told by the owl was *meant* to sound further-off and more like an ordinary fairy-tale so as to keep it different from the part where I get on to telling it myself. I think the *idea* of making some difference is right: but of course what matters in books is not so much the ideas as how you actually carry them out.

All good wishes and love to both,

yours
C. S. Lewis

❖

Dec[ember] 18th. [19]53

Dear Phyllida

Thanks for your most interesting cards. How do you get the *gold* so good? Whenever I tried to use it, however golden it looked on the shell, it always looked only like rough brown on the paper. Is it that you have some trick with the brush that I never learned, or that gold paint is better now than when I was a boy! The "conversation-piece" (I think that is what the art critics w[oul]d. call your group) is excellent and most interesting. If you hadn't told me your Father was mixing putty I sh[oul]d. have thought he was mixing colours on a palette, but otherwise everything explains itself. I never saw a family who all had such a likeness to their Mother.

I'm not quite sure what you meant about "silly adventure stories without my point". If they *are* silly, then having a point won't save them. But if they are good in themselves, and if by a "point" you mean some truth about the real world wh.[ich] one can take *out of* the story, I'm not sure that I agree. At least, I think that *looking for* a "point" in that sense may prevent one sometimes from getting the real effect of the story in itself—like listening too hard for the words in singing which isn't meant to be listened to that way (like an anthem in a chorus). I'm not at all sure about all this, mind you: only thinking as I go along. We have two American boys in the house at present, aged 8 and 6½.[7] Very nice. They seem to use much longer words than English boys of that age would: not showing off, but just because they don't seem to know the short words. But they haven't as good table manners as English boys of the same sort would.

Well—all good wishes to you all for Christmas, and very many thanks.

yours
C. S. Lewis

P. S. Of course you're right about the Narnian books being better than the tracts; at least, in the way a picture is better than a map.

❖

[16 January 1954]

My dear Sarah

Thanks for your most interesting letter. It sounds as if you were having a much nicer time at school than most of us remember having, and if you reply "I should hope so too," well, I can't agree with you more. I particularly envy you having half a pony and

---

[7]David and Douglas Gresham were visiting the Lewis brothers with their mother, Joy. They later became Lewis's stepsons. (See Foreword.)

learning to ride. I can't, but I love the sight and sound and smell and feel of a horse and v.[ery] much wish that I could. I'd sooner have a nice, thickset, steady-going cob that knew me & that I knew how to ride than all the cars and private planes in the world.

I've been reading *Pride and Prejudice*[8] on and off all my life and it doesn't wear out a bit. Lamb, too.[9] You'll find his letters as good as his essays: indeed they are almost exactly the same, only more of it.

I don't believe anyone is "good" or "bad" at languages. If you ever want really badly to read something which you can't get in English, you'll find you can learn a foreign language alright. I liked the account of y[ou]r. XII Night Party, a ceremony I knew nothing about. Where I grew up the great thing was Halloween (eve of All Saints' Day). There was always a slightly eerie, spooky feeling mixed with games, events, and various kinds of fortune telling—*not* a good night on which to walk through a churchyard. (Tho' in fact Irish people, believing in both, are much *more* afraid of fairies than of ghosts).

I've been having a sebacious (no, not Herbacious) cyst lanced on the back of my neck: the most serious result is that I can never at present get my whole head & shoulders under water in my bath. (I like getting down like a Hippo with only my nostrils out). Give my love to all and I hope you'll have a grand year in 1954.

Yours
C. S. Lewis

[8] *Pride and Prejudice*, a novel by Jane Austen (1775–1817).
[9] Charles Lamb (1775–1834), essayist and poet.

[This letter is to an American family of eight brothers and sisters who lived in Washington, D.C. They first wrote to Lewis at the encouragement of their "Aunt Mary Willis," a family friend and the "lady" from C. S. Lewis's *Letters to an American Lady*, edited by Clyde S. Kilby (Grand Rapids, Michigan: William B. Eerdmans, 1967).]

[24 January 1954]

Dear Hugh, Anne, Noelie (There is a name I never heard before; what language is it, and does it rhyme with *oily* or *mealy* or *Kelly* or *early* or *truly*?), Nicholas, Martin, Rosamund, Matthew, and Miriam—

Thank you very much for all the lovely letters and pictures. You don't say who did the coloured one of Ransom being paddled by the Hross.[10] Hugh? I liked it. That's very much what a Hross is like but a bit too fat. And I don't know who did the one of the Prince fighting the Serpent: but it's a fine snaky snake. (I was born in Holy Ireland where there are no snakes because, as you know, St. Patrick sent them all away.) And I think Nicholas's picture of the Prince and Jill and the Chair very good—especially the Prince's legs, for legs aren't too easy to draw, are they? Noelie's White Witch is superb!—just as proud and wicked as I meant her to be. And Nicholas's other one of *The L.*[*ion*], *the W.*[*itch*], *and the W.*[*ardrobe*], (I can't write it all out!) is a nice *deep* picture, going away into the distance. Thank you all.

I have done lots of dish-washing in my time and I have often been read to, but I never thought of your

[10]Characters from the first book of Lewis's science fiction trilogy, *Out of the Silent Planet* (1938).

very sensible idea of doing both together. How many plates do you smash in a month?

There is no snow here yet and it is so warm that the foolish snowdrops and celandines (little yellow flowers; I don't know if you have them or not) are coming up as if it was spring. And squirrels (we have hundreds and thousands about this college) have never gone to bed for their winter sleep at all. I keep on warning them that they really ought to and that they'll be dreadfully sleepy (yawning their heads off) by June if they don't, but they take no notice.

You *are* a fine big family! I sh[oul]d. think your mother sometimes feels like the Old-Woman-who-lived-in-a-Shoe (you know that rhyme!). I'm so glad you like the books. The next one, *The Horse and His Boy* will be out quite soon. There are to be 7 altogether. Lots of love.

yours ever
C. S. Lewis

❖

[30 January 1954]

Dear Hila

Upon my word, a statue of Reepicheep.[11] He stares at me from my mantlepiece with just the right mixture of courtesy and readiness to fight. Thank you very much. It is very cold here now—not so cold as in N.Y., I expect, but then we have no central heating in

---

[11]Hila later described this Reepicheep as "a rather primitive effort stitched out of felt."

College, so my fingers are hardly able to write. I am so glad you liked the [*Silver*] *Chair*. With all good wishes,

yours ever
C. S. Lewis

❖

March 19th. 1954

[Dear Hugh, Anne, Noelie, Nicholas, Martin, Rosamund, Matthew, and Miriam]

You have sent me such a lot of treasures I don't know where to begin. Your story, Martin, is good and keeps one right to the end guessing what is really happening. I am a little bit surprised that the Policeman did not feel at all afraid of such a strange hostess. Or did he, and you didn't tell us? I think just a word about how he felt, and a name for him, are the only improvements I can suggest. The one place where you do tell us what it felt like for him ("He thought a moment") does a bit of good to the story. In Hugh's picture of the Dufflepuds what I like best (though the D's themselves are quite good) is the ship, just the right sort of ship, and the shadow of the ship, and the *windiness* of the sky. I mean, I like a picture of out-of-door things to look as if it was really out of doors—as this does. But you all seem able to do that. Nicky's Reepicheep shows the sunlight splendidly by the shadows of the trees. But what I like best of all is the "spirit of a tree". It is so beautifully wavy and graceful and is moving so. Bravo!

The typescript of *your* book went off to the publisher last week, though it will not be out till next year. It is called *The Magician's Nephew*.[12] You must have often wondered how the old Professor in *The Lion, [the] W[itch], [& the] W[ardrobe]* could have believed all the children told him about Narnia. The reason was that he had been there himself as a little boy. This book tells you how he went there, and (of course that was ages and ages ago by Narnian time) how he saw Aslan *creating* Narnia, and how the White Witch first got into that world and why there was a lamp-post in the middle of that forest. The one *before* yours (*The Horse and His Boy*) is also dedicated to two Americans[13] and will be out "this Autumn" (Fall, as you say). It is still cold here but the snowdrops, crocuses, primroses and daffodils are up and the thrushes are building nests. Love to all,

Yours ever
C. S. Lewis

[This letter from C. S. Lewis to a young American girl was the first of twenty-eight letters written over nearly twenty years. Joan and her family lived in New York, but wintered in Florida.]

April 15th. 1954

Dear Joan . . .

Thank you very much for your kind letter with beautiful painting and interesting photo which

---

[12]Lewis dedicated *The Magician's Nephew* to this family of American children.

[13]David and Douglas Gresham.

reached me to-day. I am so glad you like the Narnian books, and it was nice of you to tell me. There are to be seven stories altogether. The ones which have already come out are

1. *The Lion, the Witch and the Wardrobe*
2. *Prince Caspian*
3. *The Voyage of the "Dawn Treader"*
4. *The Silver Chair*.

Some time this year, Number 5, *The Horse and His Boy*, will be out; and the 6th *The Magician's Nephew* has already gone to the printer (You have no idea how long it takes getting a book printed). The 7th is already written, but still only in pen-and-ink, and I have not quite decided yet what to call it. Sometimes I think of calling it *The Last King of Narnia*, and sometimes, *Night Falls on Narnia*.[14] Which do you think sounds best?

I was at a Zoo last week and saw the real lions; also some perfectly lovely bears nursing their cubs.

How lucky you are to have a pool.

With love to your brother and yourself,

yours ever
C. S. Lewis

[14]The title eventually chosen was *The Last Battle*, published in 1956.

Magdalen College,
Oxford.
28th. April 1954

Dear Hugh,

    Oh, very good. Eustace as a dragon is your best picture yet. Really awesome! Love to all.

Yours,
C. S. Lewis

❖

May 7th. 1954

Dear Joan . . . ,

    Thanks for letter and pictures. I say, you *are* lucky to have armour: I would have loved it when I was a boy but it never came my way. The kind you have would be even better for Vikings etc. than for Arthurian knights. As for doing *more* Narnian books than 7, isn't it better to stop when people are still asking for more than to go on till they are tired?

Love from,
yours
C. S. Lewis

Magdalen College,
Oxford
26th. May 1954

Dear [Hugh, Anne, Noelie, Nicholas, Martin, Rosamund, Matthew, and Miriam],

Thank both Martin and Micky for their nice letters. Do you mean Miriam *fell* into the stove? "was put
on" sounds as if you did it on purpose—were you
thinking of having her for dinner? I do hope she will
soon be better. Burns are horrid.

Yours ever,
C. S. Lewis

❖

[This letter was written to a fifth grade class in Maryland.]

Magdalen College
Oxford.
May 29th. 1954

Dear Fifth Graders

I am so glad you liked the Narnian books and it
was very kind of you to write and tell me. There are
to be 7 of them altogether and you are already one
behind. No. 4, *The Silver Chair*, is already out.

You are mistaken when you think that everything in the books "represents" something in this
world. Things do that in *The Pilgrim's Progress*[15] but
I'm not writing in that way. I did not say to myself

---

[15]*The Pilgrim's Progress*, an allegory by John Bunyan
(1628–1688).

"Let us represent Jesus as He really is in our world by a Lion in Narnia": I said "Let us *suppose* that there were a land like Narnia and that the Son of God, as He became a Man in our world, became a Lion there, and then imagine what would happen." If you think about it, you will see that it is quite a different thing. So the answer to your first two questions is that Reepicheep and Nick-i-brick don't, in that sense, represent anyone. But of course anyone in our world who devotes his whole life to seeking Heaven will be *like* R[eepicheep], and anyone who wants some worldly thing so badly that he is ready to use wicked means to get it will be likely to behave like N[ick-i-brick]. Yes, Reepicheep did get to Aslan's country. And Caspian did return safely: it says so on the last page of *The [Voyage of the] "Dawn Treader"*. Eustace did get back to Narnia, as you will find when you read *The Silver Chair*. As for who reigns in Narnia to-day, you won't know till you have had the seventh and last book.

I'm tall, fat, rather bald, red-faced, double-chinned, black-haired, have a deep voice, and wear glasses for reading.

The only way for *us* to [get to] Aslan's country is through death, as far as I know: perhaps some very good people get just a tiny glimpse before then.

Best love to you all. When you say your prayers sometimes ask God to bless me,

Yours ever,
C. S. Lewis

June 7th. 1954

Dear Joan . . . ,

Thank you for your nice letter of May 25th. I, too, like opening my eyes under water, both in the sea and in my bath; but one must not do it in a bath if it is very hot because it is bad for them.

All seven Narnian books are now written and the fifth might be out any day now. As for poems, I don't think I could do them. Some poems I did like (or would have liked) at your age are: Longfellow's *Saga of King Olaf*,[16] Matthew Arnold's *Sohrab and Rustum*,[17] Macaulay's *Lays of Ancient Rome*,[18] and G. K. Chesterton's *Ballad of the White Horse*.[19] I wonder do you like any of these.

I used to use fountain pens but somehow I don't like them now.

It is a dreadfully cold, wet summer here. The cuckoo (do you have cuckoos?) only speaks about once a day and even the squirrels are depressed.

With love,

Yours
C. S. Lewis

[16]Henry Wadsworth Longfellow (1807–1882), American poet. For Lewis's comments on the "Saga of King Olaf," see his autobiography, *Surprised by Joy: The Shape of My Early Life*, chapter one.

[17]Matthew Arnold (1822–1888), English poet and critic. See also Lewis's *Surprised by Joy*, chapter three.

[18]Thomas Babington Macaulay (1800–1859), English historian and essayist.

[19]Gilbert Keith Chesterton (1874–1936), English author and Christian apologist.

Magdalen College,
Oxford.
9th. June 1954

Dear [Hugh, Anne, Noelie, Nicholas, Martin, Rosamund, Matthew, and Miriam],

Congratulations on [your new baby sister] Deborah to you all. I like red hair. I never saw a picture of a [baby] shower before. I had to put up my umbrella to look at it. The picture of the lamp-post is good too. Tell Nicky I don't smoke cigars. Love to all.

Yours,
C. S. Lewis

❖

[12 July 1954]

Dear Joan

I am so busy marking examination papers that I can hardly breathe! The very good ones and the very bad ones are no trouble, but the in-between ones take ages. Thanks for telling me the bits you liked (Yes. I have old copies). Chautauqua sounds lovely. In great haste,

Yours ever
C. S. Lewis

Magdalen College,
Oxford.
9th. September 1954

Dear Joan,

Many thanks for your nice letter of 31st. August,
which I found most interesting. You are lucky that at
your age you are having such lovely dreams: and how
very well you describe them. This, I may add, is not
just compliment, I really mean that what you write is
good. I do see your Coloured Mountains. When I was
young, all my dreams were horrors—insects the size
of small ponies which closed in upon me, etc. I've
never seen Aida,[20] but I've known the music since I
was a small boy: and how good it is. It's rather the
fashion over here now amongst the musical snobs to
look down their noses when Verdi is mentioned and
talk about the "cheapness of his thematic material".
What they really mean is that Verdi could write *tunes*
and they can't! With love,

yours
C. S. Lewis

[20]*Aida*, an opera by Italian composer, Giuseppe Verdi
(1813–1901).

Magdalen College,
Oxford.
20th. October 1954

Dear Joan . . . ,

It was very nice of you to send me the telegram, and I am so glad you liked *The Horse and His Boy*. I was going to send this to your New York home, but I see you are still on holidays in Florida. I hope it has been nicer than my seaside holiday, when it was very cold, and rained nearly all the time.

Yours sincerely,
C. S. Lewis

❖

[In December 1954, C. S. Lewis left Magdalen College, Oxford, to accept a new position as professor of Medieval and Renaissance English at Magdalene College, Cambridge University.]

Magdalene College
Cambridge

[15 January 1955]

Dear Martin

Thanks for your nice card and letter. What would they call the last hurricanes if there were more of them than there are letters in the alphabet? I mean, after Xanthippe, Yolande, and Zena, who w[oul]d. come next? I too have been busy moving to a new job and a new home. Notice that my new college, though

pronounced like my old one (they are both called
MAUDLIN) is spelled differently: with an E at the
end. It is snowing here. Cambridge looks nice in
snow. Love to all,

Yours

C. S. Lewis

❖

[19 February 1955]

Dear Joan

I am so glad to hear that Loge is called after Loge
in *The Ring*, for I am very fond of *The Ring* myself. It
must be exciting to have a father who sings in it. Have
you got it in book form with pictures by Arthur Rackham?[21] Two lovely volumes. He does Mime specially
well.

I hope *The Magic Spoon* will be a great success. I
know what you mean about not being able to get the
mountains right in the picture. I sometimes think that
really imaginary things are better to write about than
to draw or paint; but perhaps I think that only because I can write better than I draw.

You see I have changed my job and my address.

---

[21]*The Ring of the Nibelung* is an operatic cycle based on Scan-
dinavian legend by German composer Richard Wagner
(1813–1883). Lewis first came under the spell of Arthur Rackham's
illustrations to this work when he was a boy. (Rackham had illustrated Margaret Armour's two-volume adaptation of Wagner,
Siegfried and the Twilight of the Gods and *The Rhinegold and the
Valkyries*). See also Lewis's *Surprised by Joy*, chapter five.

Note the different spellings: Magdalen at Oxford and Magdalene at Cambridge. But they are both pronounced Maudlin. This is a lovely little college and looks nice to-day, all covered with snow.

With love,

Yours,
C. S. Lewis

❖

[22 February 1955]

Dear Marcia . . .

I am so glad you like the Narnian books. After *P.[rince] Caspian* came *The Voyage of the "Dawn Treader"*: Then *The Silver Chair*: then *The Horse and His Boy*. These have all been published. Next autumn, will come *The Magician's Nephew*, and, the year after, *The Last Battle* (at least I think that will be the name, but I might change it) which will finish off the series. Peter gets back to Narnia in it. I am afraid Susan does not. Haven't you noticed in the two you have read that she is rather fond of being too grownup. I am sorry to say that side of her got stronger and she forgot about Narnia.

No. I didn't start with four real children in mind: I just made them up.

It *is* fun writing stories, isn't it! Like you I used to write lots at your age.

With all good wishes,

Yours sincerely
C. S. Lewis

[When Laurence, a nine-year-old American boy, became concerned that he loved Aslan more than Jesus, his mother wrote to C. S. Lewis in care of Macmillan Publishing Company. Just ten days later to her surprise and delight, she received this answer to her son's questions.]

[6 May 1955]

Dear Mrs. K . . . ,

Tell Laurence from me, with my love:

1/ Even if he was loving Aslan more than Jesus (I'll explain in a moment why he can't really be doing this) he would not be an idol-worshipper. If he was an idol-worshipper he'd be doing it on purpose, whereas he's now doing it because he can't help doing it, and trying hard not to do it. But God knows quite well how hard we find it to love Him more than anyone or anything else, and He won't be angry with us as long as we are trying. And He will help us.

2/ But Laurence can't *really* love Aslan more than Jesus, even if he feels that's what he is doing. For the things he loves Aslan for doing or saying are simply the things Jesus really did and said. So that when Laurence thinks he is loving Aslan, he is really loving Jesus: and perhaps loving Him more than he ever did before. Of course there is one thing Aslan has that Jesus has not—I mean, the body of a lion. (But remember, if there are other worlds and they need to be saved and Christ were to save them as He would—He may really have taken all sorts of bodies in them which we don't know about.) Now if Laurence is bothered because he finds the lion-body seems nicer to him than the man-body, I don't think he *need* be bothered at all. God knows all about the way a little boy's imagination works (He made it, after all) and knows that at a certain age the idea of talking and friendly animals is very attractive. So I don't think He minds if Laurence likes the Lion-body. And anyway, Laurence will find as he grows older, that feeling (liking the lion-body better) will die away of itself, without his taking any trouble about it. So he needn't bother.

3/ If I were Laurence I'd just say in my prayers something like this: "Dear God, if the things I've been thinking and feeling about those books are things You don't like and are bad for me, please take away those feelings and thoughts. But if they are not bad, then please stop me from worrying about them. And help me every day to love you more in the way that really matters far more than any feelings or imaginations, by doing what you want and growing more like you." That is the sort of thing I think Laurence should say for himself; but it would be kind and Christian-like if he then added, "And if Mr. Lewis has worried any other children by his books or done them any harm, then please forgive him and help him never to do it again."

Will this help? I am terribly sorry to have caused such trouble, and would take it as a great favor if you would write again and tell me how Laurence goes on. I shall of course have him daily in my prayers. He must be a corker of a boy: I hope you are prepared for the possibility he might turn out a saint. I daresay the saints' mothers have, in some ways, a rough time!

Yours sincerely,
C. S. Lewis

[3 June 1955]

Dear Joan

Thanks for your letter. My college "is out" (as you say: we should say "goes down" at the universities and "breaks up" at school) by the end of next week. Yes, it has stopped snowing but this has been the latest and coldest spring I've ever known. It only began getting warm, and the cuckoo only began seriously cuckooing, about a week ago. Not that it is what you would call warm. The water in our river, the Cam, is only up to 62°. I shall go to Oxford when term is over (if I can get there. I don't drive a car—I'm no good at any sort of machine—and we're having a railway strike at the moment).

Talking about *The Ring*, there's a little old man who brings my breakfast every morning who is exactly like Mime.

I finished correcting the proofs of the last of all the Narnian books a few weeks ago, so I suppose [*The Last Battle*] will be out in autumn.

With love & good wishes,

Yours
C. S. Lewis

The Kilns
Headington Quarry,
Oxford

[20 July 1955]

Dear Hugh,

Thanks for your letter of June 14th. I am delighted to hear that you approve of *The M[agician]'s
N[ephew]*; it would have been awkward if the one dedicated to you had turned out to be just the one of the
whole series that you couldn't stand! I am thrilled to
hear that your street runs North as well as South,
because in this country *all* streets (and even country
roads) run in two directions at the same time. They
are trained to change the moment you turn around.
What is even cleverer of them they turn their right
side into their left side at the same time. I've never
known it fail.

Love to all,

Yours ever
C. S. Lewis

❖

The Kilns, Kiln Lane
Headington Quarry,
Oxford.
14th September 1955.

Dear Teensie,

(Since this is what you call yourself [Joan]), heartiest congratulation on your First Prize; and how lucky

you have been to have such a season of Opera. It must have been lovely. I don't understand your weather; does it get *cooler* in America when August comes? With us—when we have a summer, which is about once every seven years—it gets *hotter* in August. I'm very sorry indeed to hear about your father's ill-health, but delighted to know that he has recovered; and please tell him so.

I'm just back from the mountains of Donegal, which are very beautiful, and where I had some grand walks and bathes.

With love,

yours,
C. S. Lewis

❖

Magdalene College,
Cambridge

[16 October 1955]

Dear Joan

Thanks for your letter of the 3rd. In this country we hardly ever have any snow worth talking about till January, or later. Once we had it at Easter after all the trees had their spring leaves on. So the snow could lie on the trees far heavier than if they had been bare, and there was great destruction in the way of broken branches. We had our first frost last night—this morning the lawns are all grey, with a pale, bright sunshine on them: wonderfully beautiful. And somehow *exciting*. The first beginning of the winter always excites me; it makes me want adventures. I expect our autumn has gentler colours than your fall and it goes far slower. The trees, especially beeches, keep their leaves for weeks & weeks after they have begun to change colour, turning from yellow to gold & from gold to flame-colour.

I never knew a guinea-pig that took any notice of humans (they take plenty of one another). Of those small animals I think Hamsters are the most amusing—. And, to tell you the truth, I'm still fond of mice. But the guinea pigs go well with your learning German. If they talked, I'm sure that is the language they'd speak.

Yours ever
C. S. Lewis

❖

Magdalene College,
Cambridge

[24 October 1955]

My dear Laurence—I was very glad to get a letter from your Mother to-day because now I can answer one you wrote me a long time ago. The reason I could not answer you before was that the corner of your letter got wet before it reached me and the address was all blotted out so that I could not read it; so I did not know where to send my answer to. Now: I don't dislike Panthers at all, I think they are one of the loveliest animals there are. I don't remember that I have put any *bad* panthers in the books (there are some good ones fighting against Rabadash in *The Silver Chair*,[22] aren't there?) and even if I have that wouldn't mean I thought all Panthers bad, any more than I think all men bad because of Uncle Andrew, or all boys bad because Edmund was once a traitor. I'm sorry my handwriting is so hard: it was very nice until about 10 years ago, but now I have rheumatism in my wrist. Please thank your Mother for her nice letter; I enjoyed it very much. And now goodbye. Don't forget sometimes to put in a word for me when you say your prayers, and I'll do the same for you.

> yours ever
> C. S. Lewis

❖

> The Kilns,
> Headington Quarry,
> Oxford

[26 December 1955]

Dear Joan

Thanks very much for your gay card and lovely bookmarker. And 100,000 good wishes. Can't write properly—there are dreadful mails at present—I write letters all day—it spoils Christmas completely. A fox has killed one of our geese,

> Yours ever
> C. S. Lewis

[22]Rabadash is in *The Horse and His Boy*, not *The Silver Chair*, a mistake which Lewis realized only too late after mailing this letter.

The Kilns,
Headington Quarry,
Oxford

[27 December 1955]

My dear Sarah

Thank you very much for the wholly admirable mug, out of which I hope often to drink your very good health. And do you know, it reminded me that I'd completely ignored *all* my godchildren this year, which I don't think ever happened before. I *am* a Pig: *porcisscimus*. Somehow the whole horrible business of "Xmas" (which I distinguish sharply from *Christmas*), with the huge mails coming in every half hour, has quite got me down this year and I wasn't really in my right mind till yesterday evening. I now enclose a belated present.

When I last met your father and mother, *mice* were weighing rather heavily on their minds. I should think the population runs into millions by now.

Love to them (I mean your parents, tho' of course I don't mind—at a distance—including the mice too) and yourself and all good wishes for 1956,

Yours affectionately
C. S. Lewis

The Kilns,
Headington Quarry,
Oxford

[26 March 1956]

Dear Martin . . .

It was nice to hear from you, and I know very well what it's like when there's always something to do! The funny thing is that I was far worse about writing letters when I had far fewer to write; now that I have such a lot to write I've just got to do them all at once, first thing every morning.

I *am* sorry for you having been . . . bandaged all those months. Did it *itch* dreadfully under the bandage where one can't get at it? I know I did when I was bandaged for ages after my wound in the first war. But it's lovely when at last you do get it off; seeing your own skin again is almost like meeting an old friend!

I suppose your exam is all over by now. I hope you did v.[ery] well in it and that you will like the new school.

Give my love to all the others. We are all well. We're bringing up a (ginger) kitten at present and it behaves very like your [baby sister] Deborah.

Yours
C. S. Lewis

[On April 23, 1956, C. S. Lewis married Joy Davidman Gresham and became stepfather to her sons, David (age 12) and Douglas (age 10½). Just four days later, Lewis wrote this reply to his young American friend, Laurence, who had wondered why the children in *The Last Battle* were uncertain about what would happen to them if they died. Laurence went on to ask if the children did not know the Apostles' Creed, especially where it states: "I believe in . . . the resurrection of the body, and the life everlasting."]

[27 April 1956]

Dear Laurence

Thanks for your nice letter and the photograph. I am so glad you like *The Last Battle*. As to whether they knew their Creed, I suppose Professor Kirke and the Lady Polly and the Pevensies did, but probably Eustace and Pole, who had been brought up at that rotten school did *not*.

Your mother tells me you have all been having chicken pox. I had it long after I was grown up and it's much worse if you are a man for of course you can't shave with the spots on your face. So I grew a beard and though my hair is black the beard was half yellow and half red! You should have seen me.

Yes, people do find it hard to keep on feeling as if you believed in the next life: but then it is just as hard to keep on feeling as if you believed you were going to be nothing after death. I know this because in the old days before I was a Christian I used to try.

Last night a young thrush flew into my sitting room and spent the whole night there. I didn't know what to do, but in the morning one of the college servants very cleverly caught it and put it out without hurting it. Its mother was waiting for it outside and was very glad to meet it again. (By the way, I always forget which birds you have in America. Have you thrushes? They have lovely songs and speckled chests).

Good-by for the present and love to you all,

> yours sincerely
> C. S. Lewis

❖

> The Kilns,
> Headington Quarry,
> Oxford

[14 May 1956]

Dear Martin

How fine you must be feeling. Bandage off and scholarship won! Hearty congratulations on both. I hope the scholarship will be only the first of many successes.

I should jolly well think Mervin (the young cat) *has* grown up; he chases quite large dogs out of the garden now.

Thanks for photo and love to all,

> Yours
> C. S. Lewis

> The Kilns,
> Headington Quarry,
> Oxford

[26 June 1956]

Dear Joan—

Thanks for your letter of the 3rd. You describe your Wonderful Night v.[ery] well. That is, you describe the place & the people and the night and the feeling of it all, very well—but not the *thing* itself—the setting but not the jewel. And no wonder! Wordsworth[23] often does just the same. His *Prelude* (you're bound to read it about 10 years hence. Don't try it now, or you'll only spoil it for later reading) is full of moments in which everything except the *thing* itself is described. If you become a writer you'll be trying to describe the *thing* all your life: and lucky if, out of dozens of books, one or two sentences, just for a moment, come near to getting it across.

About *amn't I, aren't I*, and *am I not*, of course there are no right and wrong answers about language in the sense in which there are right and wrong answers in Arithmetic. "Good English" is whatever educated people talk; so that what is good in one place or time w[oul]d. not be so in another. *Amn't* was good 50 years ago in the North of Ireland where I was brought up, but bad in Southern England. *Aren't I* w[oul]d. have been hideously bad in Ireland but very good in England. And of course I just don't know which (if either) is good in modern Florida. Don't take any

---

[23]William Wordsworth (1770–1850), English poet.

notice of teachers and text-books in such matters. Nor of logic. It is good to say "More than one passenger was hurt," although *more than one* equals at least two and therefore logically the verb ought to be plural *were* not singular *was*! What really matters is:—

1. Always try to use the language so as to make quite clear what you mean and make sure y[ou]r. sentence couldn't mean anything else.
2. Always prefer the plain direct word to the long, vague one. Don't *implement* promises, but *keep* them.
3. Never use abstract nouns when concrete ones will do. If you mean "More people died" don't say "Mortality rose."
4. In writing. Don't use adjectives which merely tell us how you want us to *feel* about the thing you are describing. I mean, instead of telling us a thing was "terrible," describe it so that we'll be terrified. Don't say it was "delightful"; make *us* say "delightful" when we've read the description. You see, all those words (horrifying, wonderful, hideous, exquisite) are only like saying to your readers "Please will you do my job for me."
5. Don't use words too big for the subject. Don't say "infinitely" when you mean "very"; otherwise you'll have no word left when you want to talk about something *really* infinite.

Thanks for the photos. You and Aslan both look v.[ery] well. I hope you'll like your new home.

With love,
yours
C. S. Lewis

The Kilns, Kiln Lane,
Headington Quarry,
Oxford.
23rd July 1956.

Dear Martin,

Thank you for your letter of the 18th, it was nice to hear all your news. I hope Nicky and Noelie will enjoy Canada. We have been bringing up a new kitten (marmalade coloured) and he seems to be starting in life well; at least he has already chased a strange dog out of the garden. It has been a rotten summer here so far—temperatures down to 50, and so dark it might be December.

Love and good wishes to all.

Yours
C. S. Lewis

❖

Dec[ember] 28th. 1956

Dear Joan

Thank you very much for your beautiful picture. Unfortunately that sentence (the one I've just written) is what I should have had to say, out of politeness, even if it had been a horrid picture! That's the worst (even of "white") lies; when you *really* mean that a present is beautiful, there is nothing left to say. But this picture really *is* very good; the design good and the colour even better. What is it done in? It doesn't look either like oils or like water colours. The effect is wonderfully deep, rich, and attractive.

We have had a snowy Christmas here, which is unusual in England, but to-day it is being all washed away by rain; horrid under-foot.

All good wishes for the New Year,

Yours
C. S. Lewis

❖

Dec[ember] 30th. 1956

My dear Sarah

Thank you for the beautiful little jar. I am trying to think of some treasure choice enough to put in it. I am also v.[ery] ashamed of not having sent you a card this Christmas. But I've really been snowed under. All domestic help was away for its holidays. I have a sick (v.[ery] sick) wife[24] to visit daily in hospital. At home I had to look after a sick[x] brother, 2 schoolboy stepsons, one dog, one cat, four geese, umpteen hens, two stoves, three pipes in danger of freezing; so I was pretty busy and pretty tired. Well, all good wishes to all of you and here's a new-year's gift.

With Love
C. S. Lewis

[x]SICK. It looks like RICH (he isn't!)

[24]Joy Lewis was seriously ill with cancer.

[22 January 1957]

Dear Martin

The books don't tell us what happened to Susan. She is left alive in this world at the end, having by then turned into a rather silly, conceited young woman. But there is plenty of time for her to mend, and perhaps she will get to Aslan's country in the end—in her own way. I think that whatever she had seen in Narnia she *could* (if she was the sort that wanted to) persuade herself, as she grew up, that it was "all nonsense."

Congratulations on your good marks. I wish I was good at Maths! Love to all,

Yours
C. S. Lewis

❖

The Kilns, Kiln Lane,
Headington Quarry,
Oxford.
13th April 1957.

My dear Penny,

Thanks for your letter and the pictures. You draw donkeys better than Pauline Baynes[25] does. I am so glad you like the book. Please give my greetings and deep thanks to your father and mother. They will

[25]Lewis chose Pauline Baynes to illustrate his *Chronicles of Narnia* after he admired the artwork she had done for J. R. R. Tolkien's *Farmer Giles of Ham* (1949).

understand that I have hardly time to live at present, let alone write a decent letter.

With love,

yours,
Jack

❖

April 23rd. [19]57

Dear Laurence

I think I agree with your order for reading the books more than with your mother's.[26] The series was not planned beforehand as she thinks. When I wrote *The Lion*, [*the Witch, and the Wardrobe*] I did not know I was going to write any more. Then I wrote *P.[rince] Caspian* as a sequel and still didn't think there would be any more, and when I had done *The Voyage* [*of the "Dawn Treader"*] I felt quite sure it would be the last. But I found I was wrong. So perhaps it does not matter very much in which order anyone reads them. I'm not even sure that all the others were written in the same order in which they were published. I never

---

[26]Laurence's mother felt that the seven *Chronicles of Narnia* should be read in the order in which they were published, since she assumed that this sequence was intentional. Laurence, however, believed that the stories should be read chronologically according to Narnian time: *The Magician's Nephew*, *The Lion, the Witch and the Wardrobe*, *The Horse and His Boy*, *Prince Caspian*, *The Voyage of the "Dawn Treader," The Silver Chair*, and *The Last Battle*.

Lewis later reaffirmed his preference for Laurence's sequence. See Walter Hooper, *Past Watchful Dragons* (New York: Collier Books/Macmillan Publishing Co., 1979), p. 32.

keep notes of that sort of thing and never remember dates.

Well, I can't say I have had a happy Easter, for I have lately got married and my wife is very, very ill. I am sure Aslan knows best and whether He leaves her with me or takes her to His own country, He will do what is right. But of course it makes me very sad. I am sure you and your mother will pray for us.

All good wishes to you both.

yours
C. S. Lewis

❖

The Kilns, Kiln Lane,
Headington Quarry,
Oxford.
25th April 1957.

Dear Joan,

Very nice to hear from you again after this long time. No, I've never had the chance to go to Bayreuth,[27] though of course I've heard the Ring at Covent Garden; but I'm sure that is not at all the same thing, and I envy you your good luck; and as for the Flying Dutchman,[28] my hearing of it has been limited to gramophone records. My German is of the kindergarten variety I'm afraid; I don't speak it, and can

[27]The music festival at Bayreuth, Germany, where Richard Wagner's operas are performed.

[28]*The Flying Dutchman*, an opera based on a legendary ghost ship off the Cape of Good Hope, by Richard Wagner.

only read it with a dictionary at my elbow; I wish I did, for not to know German well is a considerable handicap I find.

I understand quite well what you mean by being "outside" yourself, and it is not, I think, a common experience; the ordinary person probably never sees the world except from inside outwards, i.e. is not able to see him or herself objectively.

Our spring over here is a wonderful one; so hot by our standards—every day temperatures of 58–66. And the flowers and the bird music are a treat.

Best of luck with the Latin,

> yours,
> C. S. L.

❖

> The Kilns,
> Headington Quarry,
> Oxford

July 10th. [19]57

Dear Martin

It was nice to hear from you again. The *eldila* are meant to be angels, not fairies. Haven't you noticed that they are always about Maledil's business? I admit I made the birth-rates of the Hrossa a bit *too* low: but of course you must remember I was picturing a world in its extreme old age—like an old man tranquilly and happily proceeding to his end.[29]

---

[29]Characters from C. S. Lewis's first science fiction novel, *Out of the Silent Planet* (1938).

I hope you are all well. That is splendid about Annie's poetry prize: give her my heartiest congratulations.

I've been rather ill with a bad back but it is slowly mending. We've been having what *we* call a heat wave, though you Virginians w[oul]d. probably call it cool enough.

Love to all,

yours
C. S. Lewis

❖

The Kilns
Headington Quarry,
Oxford

July 18 / [19]57

Dear Joan

They tell me that one sh[oul]d. never try to learn Spanish and Italian at the same time. The fact that they are so alike of course helps one a bit over the meanings of words (but Latin w[oul]d. help you almost equally for both) but it makes a confusion in one's mind about grammar and idioms—in the end one makes a horrid soup out of both. I don't know Spanish, but I know there are lovely things in Italian to read. You'll like Boiardo, Ariosto, and Tasso.[30] By the way good easy Latin reading to keep one's Latin up with is the New Testament in Latin. Any Roman

[30]Italian poets, Matteo Maria Boiardo (1441–1494), Lodovico Ariosto (1474–1533), and Torquato Tasso (1544–1595).

Catholic bookshop will have one: say you want a copy of the "Vulgate (VULGATE) New Testament." *Acts* goes specially well in Latin.

I don't think being good *always* goes with having fun: a martyr being tortured by Nero, or a resistance movement man refusing to give away his friends when tortured by the Germans, were being good but not having fun. And even in ordinary life there are things that w[oul]d. be fun to me but I mustn't do them because they w[oul]d. spoil other people's fun. But *of course* you are quite right if you mean that giving up fun for no reason except that you think it's "good" to give it up, is all nonsense. Don't the ordinary old rules about telling the truth and doing as you'd be done by tell one pretty well which kinds of fun one may have and which not? But provided the thing is in itself right, the more one likes it and the less one has to "try to be good," the better. A *perfect* man w[oul]d. never act from sense of duty; he'd always *want* the right thing more than the wrong one. Duty is only a substitute for love (of God and of other people), like a crutch, which is a substitute for a leg. Most of us need the crutch at times; but of course it's idiotic to use the crutch when our own legs (our own loves, tastes, habits etc) can do the journey on their own!

With love,

Yours
C. S. Lewis

The Kilns,
Headington Quarry,
Oxford

Aug[ust] 7th. 1957

Dear Anne and Martin
      The view that angels have no bodies of any kind has not always been held among Christians. The older idea (early Middle Ages) was that they had bodies of aether as we have bodies of gross matter. The opposite view (your one) was that of the great scholastics—Albertus Magnus,[31] Thomas Aquinas[32] etc. The old one was temporarily revived at the Renaissance by Italians like Ficino.[33] Of course I just took, for purposes of a story, the one that seemed most imaginable. I have no scruples about this because, religiously, the question seems to me of no importance. And anyway what do we mean by "matter"?
      I am so glad you both like *T[ill] W[e] H[ave] F[aces]*.[34] I think it much my best book but not many people agree.
      Hearty congratulations to Martin on his successes in Latin. Keep it up. To be able to read Latin easily (i.e. without having to translate it mentally as you go along) is an enormous advantage later on. Practice on the Latin *New Testament* where you know

[31]Albertus Magnus (1200–1280), German theologian and philosopher.
[32]Saint Thomas Aquinas (1225–1274), Italian theologian.
[33]Masilio Ficino (1433–1499), Italian philosopher.
[34]*Till We Have Faces: A Myth Retold* (1956), a novel based on the Greek myth of Cupid and Psyche.

the story already and the style is very simple. *Acts* goes especially well in St. Jerome's Latin.

The dragon in *Beowulf*[35] certainly has wings. Shooting stars were often called fire-dragons in the Middle Ages and no one w[oul]d. have called them that unless he thought dragons flew. There might be a wingless variety as well, no doubt.

Why do I not care for Plutarch,[36] I wonder? I've tried him many times, but I somehow don't get on.

I think, Anne, the 3 sisters are not v.[ery] like goddesses. They're just human souls. Psyche has a vocation and becomes a saint. Orual lives the practical life and is, after many sins, saved. As for Redival[37]— well, we'll all hope the best for everyone!

My bones feel a bit better now that I've got what they call a "surgical belt". It's really like your grandmother's corsets. It gives me a wonderful schoolboy figure!

Love to all,

Yours
C. S. Lewis

[35]*Beowulf*, a Saxon English poem dated as early as A.D. 700.
[36]Plutarch (ca. A.D. 46–120), Greek philosopher and biographer.
[37]Characters from *Till We Have Faces*.

The Kilns
Headington Quarry,
Oxford

[14 September 1957]

Dear Lucy . . . ,

I am so glad you like the Narnian stories and it was nice of you to write and tell me. I love E. Nesbit[38] too and I think I have learned a lot from her about how to write stories of this kind. Do you know Tolkien's *The Lord of the Rings*?[39] I think you w[oul]d. like it. I am also bad at Maths and it is a continual nuisance to me—I get muddled over my change in shops. I hope you'll have better luck and get over the difficulty! It makes life a lot easier.

It makes me, I think, more humble than proud to know that Aslan has allowed me to be the means of making Him more real to you. Because He could have used anyone—as He made a donkey preach a good sermon to Balaam.[40]

Perhaps, in return, you will sometimes say a prayer for me?

With all good wishes,

Yours sincerely,
C. S. Lewis

[38]Edith Nesbit (1858–1924), novelist and author of children's books. See also Lewis's *Surprised by Joy*, chapter one.

[39]*The Lord of the Rings*, a fantasy trilogy by J. R. R. Tolkien (1892–1973), professor of English Literature at Merton College, Oxford.

[40]Numbers 22: 21–41.

Dec[ember] 23rd. 1957

Dear Laurence

It is lovely to hear that you still enjoy the Narnian stories. I hope you are all well. I forget how much of my news you and your mother know. It is wonderful. Last year I married, at her bedside in hospital, a woman who seemed to be dying: so you can imagine it was a sad wedding. But Aslan has done great things for us and she is now walking about again, showing the doctors how wrong they were, and making me very happy. I was also ill myself but am now better. Good wishes to you all.

yours
C. S. Lewis

❖

As from Magdalene College,
Cambridge

Feb[ruary] 9th. 1958

Dear Joan

Thank you for the poems. I thought them very nice and quite agree with what they say. I liked the one called *Hope* best. I shall be glad when people begin talking about other things than Sputniks, won't you? One gets quite sick of the whole subject. The pity is that some cosmic rays didn't produce a muta-tion in the dog which would have made it super-rational: then it might have found its way back alive and started taking revenge on the humans!

Happy New Year.

yours
C. S. Lewis

❖

As from Magdalene College,
Cambridge.

[20 April 1958]

Dear Joan. Thanks for your nice letter of the—hullo, you haven't dated it! And we simple souls always think of you Americans (I'm married to one now, did you know?) as being so business like. Anyway, you can drive a typewriter, which I c[oul]d. no more drive than a locomotive (I'd sooner drive the locomotive too).

The bad spring seems to be all over the world. Ours has been worse than yours in a way. Not colder of course—we never have real cold like yours—but cold for us and *dry*. The ground is parched and heaven knows when we can get anything started in the garden.

I was much interested in your account of the new school. It is nice to like anything but especially nice—almost a kind of victory—to learn to like what at first seemed hateful. I am glad you can do it, for not everybody can. I know a man who never forgives a *thing*, tho' he can forgive people. I mean, if he once had bad weather in a particular place, however nice it was in itself, he'd never go there again: and if he stubbed his toe on the threshold of Heaven itself, it w[oul]d. never, never be heaven to him again!

How I remember the pleasures of sleeping late. But they've all gone now. After *having* to get up at 7.15 for many years, I now find it almost impossible to lie in bed any later and quite impossible to sleep.

I keep on getting nice letters from young readers in America: the number of loyal Narnians seems to be increasing.

With all good wishes,

Yours
C. S. Lewis

❖

[24 April 1958]

Dear Martin

It is always nice to hear of anyone really enjoying *Perelandra*.[41] I don't think the pleasure on my part is merely vanity. I enjoyed that imaginary world so much myself that I'm glad to find anyone who has been there and liked it as much as I did—just like meeting someone who has been to a place one knows and likes in the real world.

96% is a terrific average. Keep it up.

There's just no news at all about Cambridge cats. I never see one. No news and no *mews*. But the spring

[41]*Perelandra* (1943) is the second volume in C. S. Lewis's space trilogy.

has come at last and the daffodils and primroses are out and the birds are singing. I have not heard a cuckoo yet.

Love to all.

Yours
C. S. Lewis

❖

The Kilns, Kiln Lane,
Headington Quarry,
Oxford.
21st July 1958.

Dear Martin,

You certainly are having a full life. I think all the translations of Russian novels I have read must be pretty bad. Yes—the *Christian Herald* is pretty frightful, and so apparently are its readers. I have had the stupidest letters about that article.[42]
Love to all.

Yours, in great haste,
C. S. Lewis

[42]"Will We Lose God in Outer Space?" *Christian Herald*, LXXXI (April 1958), pp. 19, 74–76. This article by C. S. Lewis was later reprinted in *The World's Last Night and Other Essays* (1960).

The Kilns,
Headington Quarry,
Oxford.

Aug[ust] 31 [19]58

Dear Joan—I am sure you had fun writing the stories. The main fault of the animal one is that you don't mix the reality and the fantasy quite in the right way. One way is Beatrix Potter's[43] or Brer Rabbit's.[44] By fantasy the animals are allowed to talk and behave in many ways like humans. But their *relations* to one another and to us remain the real ones. Rabbits are in danger from foxes and men. The other way is mine: you go right out of this world into a different creation, where there are a different sort of animals. Yours are all in the real world with a real eclipse. But they don't have the real relations to one another—real small animals w[oul]d. not be friends with an owl, nor w[oul]d. it know more astronomy than they! The spy story is better but you *are* trying to get too much into the space. One feels crowded. And wouldn't the police be rather silly if they thought a man who sang the part of Wotan (how I love it, by the way) well couldn't be a spy? I hope you don't mind me telling you all this? One can learn only by seeing one's mistakes.

[43]Beatrix Potter (1866–1943), author and illustrator of *Peter Rabbit* and other children's stories. Lewis had enjoyed these books (especially *Squirrel Nutkin*) when he was a boy. See also Lewis's *Surprised by Joy*, chapter one.

[44]Brer Rabbit is a character in *Uncle Remus and His Friends* by Joel Chandler Harris (1848–1908).

We've had a terrible dark, wet summer here but it looks as if we are now beginning a nice autumn.

With love,

Yours
C. S. Lewis

P. S. The *content* of the poem is good but the verse "creaks" a bit!

❖

The Kilns,
Headington Quarry,
Oxford

[11 September 1958]

Dear [Lucy]—You've got it exactly right. A strict allegory is like a puzzle with a solution: a great romance is like a flower whose smell reminds you of something you can't quite place. I think the something is "the whole *quality* of life as we actually experience it." You can have a realistic story in which all the things and people are exactly like those we meet in real life, but the quality, the feel or texture or smell, of it is not. In a great romance it is just the opposite. I've never met Orcs or Ents or Elves[45]—but the feel of it, the sense of a huge past, of lowering danger, of heroic tasks achieved by the most apparently unheroic peo-

[45]Inhabitants of Middle-earth from Tolkien's fantasy, *The Lord of the Rings*.

ple, of distance, vastness, strangeness, homeliness (all blended together) is so exactly what living feels like to me. Particularly the heart-breaking quality in the most beautiful places, like Lothlorien.[46] And it is so like the real history of the world: "Then, as now, there was a growing darkness and great deeds were done that were not *wholly* in vain". Neither optimism (this is the last war and after it all will be lovely forever) nor pessimism (this is the last war and all civilization will end), you notice. No. The darkness comes again and again and is never wholly triumphant nor wholly defeated.

Yours sincerely,
C. S. Lewis

❖

The Kilns,
Headington Quarry,
Oxford.

Sept[ember] 29th. 1958

Dear Martin

Thanks for your letter, and *fortissimo* congratulations on Miriam's recovery. Also on escaping Cicero,[47] who, to my mind, is the greatest bore (except possibly

[46]Lothlorien, an ancient forest in Middle-earth where the golden Mallorn trees grew, from *The Lord of the Rings*.
[47]Marcus Tullius Cicero (106–43 B.C.), Roman philosopher and statesman.

Ben Jonson,[48] Launcelot Andrewes,[49] and Mrs. Humphrey Ward[50]) of all authors whether ancient or modern. You seem to be doing a pretty wide curriculum; too wide in my opinion. All schools, both here and in America, ought to teach far fewer subjects and teach them far better. We're all well. Love to everyone.

Yours
C. S. Lewis

❖

Magdalene College,
Cambridge.

Nov[ember] 23 [19]58

Dear Martin

I am so sorry to hear about Miriam's nephritis. Please give her and everyone else my sympathy. It sounds to me as if all had a good time with that Latin master, leading him on to talk of everything under the sun—especially when you don't want him to ask awkward questions, eh? It's a fine old game and we have all played it. But beware of the Maths. master who over-marks the work. Generous marking is nice

[48]Ben [Benjamin] Jonson (1572–1637), English poet and dramatist.
[49]Launcelot Andrewes (1555–1626), English scholar and prelate.
[50]Mrs. Humphrey Ward (1851–1920), English novelist, social critic, and journalist.

for the moment, but it can lead to disappointments when, later, one comes up against the real thing. American university teachers have told me that most of their freshmen come from schools where the standard was far too low and therefore think themselves far better than they really are. This means that they lose heart (and their tempers too) when told, as they have to be told, their real level.

Yours

C. S. Lewis

❖

The Kilns,
Headington Quarry,
Oxford

Jan[uary] 3, 1959

Dear Martin

I say, I had no idea what a distinguished lot [your family is]; a "nest of singing birds". More power to your elbows!

The plan of the pentameter is

$$\bar{-}\,\smile\smile\,/\,\bar{-}\,\smile\smile\,/\,\bar{-}\,\|\,\bar{-}\,\smile\smile\,/\,\bar{-}\,\smile\smile\,/\,\bar{\smile}$$

In Bird the last ∪— always is one word. That is, you c[oul]d. end up *grāt ŭs ĕ/rām* or *Ōreăs ă/bēst*, but not *ūndĭqŭe / nūne* or *cōntĭcŭ/ĭt*. Here's one in English—
Christopher eats grill'd steaks gloomily; fried he
prefers.

Yes, understanding without translating is the thing for private reading; it won't do in exams. But translating can be fun; seeing how to sound perfectly natural English *and* keep close to the Latin at the same time.

Please thank Miriam for her lively picture.

Surprised by J[oy] may get dull (I of course wouldn't know) after Wyvern,[51] but certainly *not* because *I* had lost interest. Remember this if you ever become a critic: say what the work is like, but if you start explaining *how it came* to be like that (in other words, inventing the history of the composition) you will nearly always be wrong.

Love to all,

Yours
C. S. Lewis

❖

The Kilns
Headington Quarry
Oxford

[27 March 1959]

Dear Martin,

Thanks for your letter of the 15th. You don't tell me how your sister is; be sure to mention this the next time you write. I think your proposed metre is far too

[51]*Surprised by Joy: The Shape of My Early Life* (1955) was C. S. Lewis's autobiography. Wyvern (Lewis's pseudonym for Malvern) is the preparatory school where Lewis was sent in January 1911. See *Surprised by Joy*, chapter four.

rollicking and comic for any original in so solemn a metre as the Virgilian hexameter.[52] To such a time as yours I would put only words like

"A pound of that cheese and an ounce of the butter,"

Aeneas replied with his usual stutter.

I'd like to do the *Aeneid*[53] into rhyming Alexandrines ($\cup - \cup - \cup - \cup - \cup - \cup$) but *without* a regular break in the middle as classical French has. This w[oul]d. give them the v.[ery] Virgilian quality of sounding almost like prose in the middle while the end of each line keeps them in order—e.g. I 32–3

Leading them far, far-wandered, over alien foam
—So mighty was the labour of the birth of Rome.

I can't give you the low-down on St. Michael's or Toronto. Lovely spring weather to-day (Good Friday) as it is nearly every year. Love to all,

Yours
C. S. Lewis

[52]Virgilian hexameter is the six-foot dactylic line of Greek (Virgilian) epic poetry, e.g., the *Aeneid*.
[53]The *Aeneid* was written by the Roman poet Virgil (70–19 B.C.)

> The Kilns,
> Headington Quarry,
> Oxford

[20 April 1959]

Dear Joan

Hurrah! The essay on Easter is a promising bit of work; the sentences are clear and taut and don't sprawl. You'll be able to write prose alright. As for what you are saying, I think you are exaggerating a bit at the end. Everything I need is in my soul? The Heck it is! Or if so, it must contain a great many virtues and a great deal of wisdom which neither I nor anyone else could ever find there. Very little of what I need is at present in my soul. I mean, even things of the soul's own sort, like humility or truthfulness. And it certainly does not in any obvious sense contain a number of other things which I need at the moment: e.g. a stamp for this letter. Never exaggerate. Never say more than you really mean.

The Dream is the better of the two poems, chiefly because of the line "But Mechta shall orbit the sun." I don't, honestly, think the other gains anything by being printed as verse. You know, my dear, it's only doing you harm to write *vers libre*. After you have been writing strict, rhyming verse for about 10 years it will be time to venture on the free sort. At present it only encourages you to write prose not so good as your ordinary prose and type it like verse. Sorry to be a pig!

I am so glad you like *Till We Have Faces*, because

so few people do. It is my biggest "flop" for years, and so of course *I* think it my best book.

I envy you your tour. It must be a wonderful car to climb a fire-tower! . . . or have I misunderstood. Nor do I know what a fire-tower is. But as we have water towers here, I suppose other countries may have fire-, earth-, and air-, towers.

We are having a very cold, wet spring, but are all well.

Yours
C. S. Lewis

❖

The Kilns,
Headington Quarry,
Oxford

11 Aug[ust] 1959

Dear Joan

Congratulations on your 98% in Latin. What a drole idea in Florida, to give credits not for what you know but for hours spent in a classroom! Rather like judging the condition of an animal not by its weight or shape but by the amount of food that had been offered it!

A story about Caesar in Gaul sounds very promising. Have you read Naomi Mitchison's *The Conquered*?[54] And if not, I wonder should you? It might be

[54]*The Conquered*, a historical novel of ancient Rome by Naomi Mitchison (1897-   ), a classical scholar and author.

too strong an influence if you did (at any rate until your own book is nearly finished). On the other hand, you may need to read it in order to avoid being at any point too like it without knowing you are doing so. I don't know what one sh[oul]d. read on Gaul. Apart from archaeological finds . . . I suppose Caesar himself is our chief evidence? He will be great fun and I hope you will enjoy yourself thoroughly. Which side will you be on? I'm all for the Gauls myself and I hate all conquerors. But I never knew a woman who was not all for Caesar—just as they were in his life-time.

One of our rare really hot English summers this year.

Sorry the previous page is such a mess. I mistook a piece of ordinary paper for blotting paper!

With all good wishes,

Yours
C. S. Lewis

❖

The Kilns,
Headington Quarry,
Oxford

18 Aug[ust] 1959

Dear Martin—Don't bother about Alanus.[55] The prophecies of Merlin are much the least interesting

---

[55]Alanus de Insulis, or Alain de Lille (1128–1202), French poet and theologian.

thing about him. The fullest source for the Merlin story is the prose *Merlin*.[56] The medieval English translation of this (several volumes) was published by the Early English Text Society. You are not likely to find it except in a university library. You have Geoffrey.[57] A v.[ery] good source, if you can get hold of it, is *Arthurian Chronicles from Wace and Layamon* by Eugene Mason,[58] published by Dents of London many years ago in the series called the Everyman Library. The Layamon part is the part worth reading. The full text of Layamon was also done in 3 vols. by Sir Charles Madder[59] and had a trans. into modern English at the bottom of the page—but it is by now a very rare book. The big 3 vol. *Works of Sir Thomas Malory* edited by E. Vinaver[60] w[oul]d. be easier to come by, and perhaps by assiduously going through his notes wherever Merlin is mentioned (begin from the index of course) you might find some helpful facts.

I am so very glad to hear of your sister's recovery. All the best.

Yours
C. S. Lewis

[56]*Merlin* (1886), a work edited by G. Paris and J. Ulrich.

[57]Geoffrey of Monmouth (1100?–1154), *History of the Kings of Britain*.

[58]*Arthurian Chronicles*, edited by Eugene Mason, English author and translator, was first published in the Everyman's Library edition in 1912.

[59]The evidence suggests that rather than Sir Charles Madder, Lewis is referring to Frederick Madden's three-volume edition of Layamon's *Brut* (1847).

[60]*The Works of Sir Thomas Malory* (1947), edited by Eugene Vinaver.

18 Nov[ember] 1959

Dear [Hugh]

I meant only to deal with that particular argument, which, as you rightly say, has been used by Fundamentalists (and Calvinists) as well as by Rome. I was not proposing a discussion on the Roman position in general. Indeed if Faith . . . in the Church of Rome only comes by supernatural gift, there is not much room for discussion.

All the best,

Yours
C. S. Lewis

❖

The Kilns, Kiln Lane,
Headington Quarry,
Oxford.
25th December 1959.

Dear Joan . . . ,

Many thanks for your card; I wish you all possible happiness in the coming year.

Yours sincerely,
C. S. Lewis

5 Feb[ruary] 1960

Dear Susan . . .

All I can tell you is that pictures come into my head and I write stories about them. I don't know how or why the pictures come. I don't think I could write a *play* to save my life. I am so glad you like the Narnian books. Remember me to David D. . . .

Yours

C. S. Lewis

❖

[The oldest in a family of seven girls, Patricia was thirteen and lived in Surrey when she wrote to Lewis.]

8 June 1960

Dear [Patricia]

All your points are in a sense right. But I'm not exactly "representing" the real (Christian) story in symbols. I'm more saying "Suppose there were a world like Narnia and it needed rescuing and the Son of God (or the 'Great Emperor oversea') went to redeem *it*, as He came to redeem ours, what might it, in that world, all have been like?" Perhaps it comes to much the same thing as you thought, but not quite.

1. The creation of Narnia is the Son of God creating *a* world (not specially *our* world).

2. Jadis plucking the apple is, like Adam's sin, an act of disobedience, but it doesn't fill the same place in

her life as his plucking did in his. She was *already* fallen (very much so) before she ate it.

3. The stone table *is* meant to remind one of Moses' table.

4. The Passion and Resurrection of Aslan are the Passion and Resurrection Christ might be supposed to have had in *that* world—like those in our world but not exactly like.

5. Edmund is like Judas a sneak and traitor. But unlike Judas he repents and is forgiven (as Judas no doubt w[oul]d. have been if he'd repented).

6. Yes. At the v.[ery] *edge* of the Narnian world Aslan begins to appear more like Christ as He is known in *this* world. Hence, the Lamb. Hence, the breakfast—like at the end of St. John's Gospel. Does not He say "You have been allowed to know me in *this* world (Narnia) so that you may know me better when you get back to your own"?

7. And of course the Ape and Puzzle, just before the last Judgement (in the *Last Battle*) are like the coming of Antichrist before the end of our world.

All clear?

I'm so glad you like the books.

Yours sincerely
C. S. Lewis

[By 1960, C. S. Lewis had been writing to his goddaughter, Sarah, for sixteen years.]

21 Nov[ember] 1960

My dear Sarah

A hundred thousand congratulations and blessings. I hope you will be very happy indeed. The Lieutenant sounds all he ought to be—tho' I rather regret the evolutionary process which has turned sea-dogs into salt horses! I couldn't come to the wedding, my dear. I haven't the pluck. Any wedding, for the reason you know, would turn me inside out now.[61] I send a little present. All blessings, and love to your mother and father.

Yours ever
C. S. Lewis

❖

As from Magdalene College,
Cambridge

6 Dec[ember] 1960

Dear [Meredith],

1. Why did I become a writer? Chiefly, I think, because my clumsiness or fingers prevented me from making things in any other way. See my *Surprised by Joy*, chapter I.

[61]After her long illness with cancer, Joy Lewis died on July 13, 1960.

2. What "inspires" my books? Really I don't know. Does anyone know where exactly an idea comes from? With me all fiction *begins with* pictures in my head. But where the pictures come from I couldn't say.

3. Which of my books do I think most "representational"? Do you mean (a.) Most representative, most typical, most characteristic? or (b.) Most full of "representations" i.e. images. But whichever you mean, surely this is a question not for me but for my readers to decide. Or do you mean simply which do I like best? Now, the answer w[oul]d. be *Till We Have Faces* and *Perelandra*.

4. I have, as usual, dozens of "plans" for books, but I don't know which, if any, of these will come off. Very often a book of mine gets written when I'm tidying a drawer and come across notes for a plan rejected by me years ago and now suddenly realize I can do it after all. This, you see, makes predictions rather difficult!

5. I enjoy writing fiction more than writing anything else. Wouldn't anyone?

Good luck with your "project."

yours sincerely,
C. S. Lewis

The Kilns, Kiln Lane,
Headington Quarry,
Oxford.
26th December 1960.

Dear Joan,

How very nice to hear from you again; and
though I'm too late to wish you a merry Christmas, I
can at least hope that you will have a happy 1961.
Glad to know you've managed to get hold of a copy of
The Conquered.[62]

I suppose down in Florida you are living under
almost summer conditions; here it is dull, wet, and
warm—worst fall for 145 years in this part of the
world!

With all best wishes,

yours sincerely,
C. S. Lewis

❖

15 Feb[ruary] 1961

Dear [Hugh]

If I had time to re-read my own book (by now a
pretty old one) I'd be able to answer you better,
meanwhile:

1. Can we assume that whatever is true of the
   glorified body of our Lord is equally true of the
   glorified body of each Christian? I doubt it. His
   natural body did not undergo dissolution.

[62]See Lewis's letter of August 11, 1959, to Joan.

2. I don't quite accept the implication of your phrase "restricted by external quantity", for restriction suggests imperfection. But to be in one place (or therefore not in another) seems to me possibly hard on the perfection of a finite creature—as it belongs to the perfection of a statue to end where it does or of a musical note to be just so loud (neither more or less) or of a metrical verse.

3. I am not at all sure that blessed souls have a strictly timeless being (a *totum simal*) like God. Don't some theologians interpose *aevum* as a half-way house between *tempus* & *aeternitas*.

In general, I incline to think that tho' the blessed will participate in the Divine Nature, they will do so always in a mode which does not simply annihilate their humanity. Otherwise it is difficult to see why the species was created at all.

Of course I'm only guessing.

yours
C. S. Lewis

❖

As from Magdalene College,
Cambridge

17 Feb[ruary] 1961

Dear [Hugh]
I was so interested in the questions your last letter raised that I forgot two things I meant to say in my answer.

1. Deep sympathy on the diabetes, and thank God for insulin.

2. An appeal for your charity. [Living near you is a "lonely" and sometimes "disagreeable woman"] with whom I have corresponded for many years.[63] She is a R.[oman] C.[atholic]. . . . I have done, and am doing, what I can for her with advice and a little money. But a little help and friendship from co-religionists on the spot is badly needed. Could you, or anyone in your circle—perhaps a really nice Nun—get in touch with her and lend a hand?

yours
C. S. Lewis

❖

13 March 1961

Dear Hugh

Of course I'd quite forgotten that your family first put Mrs. S. in touch with me (and how!—the poor old soul is the lengthiest letter writer, barring the lunatics—on my list). I w[oul]d. not have mentioned her to you if I'd had the fact before me. You've done your bit. But your account raises my opinion of her; she never mentioned the old Virginian blood to me. That silence is a point in her favour.

[63]The reference here is to Aunt Mary Willis. See the note accompanying Lewis's letter of January 24, 1954, to Hugh and his brothers and sisters.

I can't possibly pursue the theological question just now, but I think the disagreement between us is less than I had supposed.

> yours
> C. S. Lewis

❖

[Jonathan wrote to Lewis from Connecticut. He noted that he was eight years old and had enjoyed all seven of the Narnian books. He also expressed his wish that: "I hope . . . you are going to write another one soon. If you don't, what am I going to read when I am nine, ten, eleven and twelve?"]

> The Kilns, Kiln Lane,
> Headington Quarry,
> Oxford.
> 29th March 1961.

Dear Jonathan . . . ,

Yours is one of the nicest letters I have had about the Narnian books, and it was very good of you to write it. But I'm afraid there will be no more of these stories. But why don't *you* try writing some Narnian tales? I began to write when I was about your age, and it was the greatest fun. Do try!

With all best wishes,

> yours sincerely,
> C. S. Lewis

The Kilns,
Headington Quarry,
Oxford

5 April 1961

Dear [Hugh]

. . . Your definition of gaiety is v.[ery] much to the point. Perhaps one can carry it further. A creature can never be a perfect *being*, but may be a perfect *creature*—e.g. a good angel or a good apple-tree. Gaiety at its highest may be an (intellectual) creature's delighted recognition that its imperfection as a being may constitute part of its perfection as an element in the whole hierarchical order of creation. I mean, while it is a pity there sh[oul]d. be bad men or bad dogs, part of the excellence of a good man is that he is *not* an angel, and of a good dog that it is *not* a man. This is an extension of what St. Paul says about the body & the members. A good toe-nail is not an unsuccessful attempt at a hair; and if it were conscious it w[oul]d. delight in being simply a good toe-nail,

yours
C. S. Lewis

The Kilns, Kiln Lane,
Headington Quarry,
Oxford.
11th January 1962

Dear Martha. . . . ,

I am so glad to hear that you liked the Narnian books, and it was very good of you to write and tell me that you did. Everyone is pleased, you know, to be appreciated, even elderly authors!
With all good wishes to you for a happy 1962,

yours sincerely,
C. S. Lewis

❖

The Kilns, Kiln Lane,
Headington Quarry,
Oxford.
14th February 1962.

Dear Sydney . . . ,

First of all I want to congratulate you on your good hand-writing, and then to tell you how glad I am that you liked my books; and it was very good of you to take the trouble to write and tell me that you did.

I'm afraid I've said all I had to say about Narnia, and there will be no more of these stories. But why don't you try to write one yourself? I was writing

stories before I was your age, and if you try, I'm sure
you would find it great fun. Do!

  With all best wishes,

yours sincerely,
C. S. Lewis

❖

The Kilns,
Headington Quarry,
Oxford

[24 March 1962]

Dear Francine

  I was at three schools (all boarding schools) of
which two were very horrid. I never hated anything
so much, not even the front line trenches in World
War I. Indeed the story is far *too* horrid to tell anyone
of your age. So glad you like the Narnian books. With
all good wishes.

yours sincerely,
C. S. Lewis

The Kilns,
Headington Quarry,
Oxford

28 March [19]62

Dear Joan

(Or are you so old that I should now call you Miss L . . . ?) It was nice to hear from you again. I am a great deal better, but apparently I shall always be rather an invalid: but it doesn't hurt, and anyway I'm 63, so I haven't much to complain of.

The imagery of your poem—what one can picture—is goodish. But the metre is surely too much of a jig for so grave a subject. Nor (forgive me!) do you handle that metre very well. You make me treat "angel throngs rush" as if it were the metrical equivalent of "Banbury Cross."[64] But *throngs* is far too long & heavy a word to be hurried over like that!

I don't know whether Lucifer & Gabriel could really find much ground for reconciliation in the mere fact that they both *exist*. I suppose the reconciliation of dark & light w[oul]d. be fog? Don't like fog much myself. Health and disease both exist in me and are now reconciled in mild invalidism. But really, I'd rather that Health had fought and slain his antagonist!

All good wishes,

Yours
C. S. Lewis

[64]"Banbury Cross" is a nursery rhyme from *Mother Goose*.

The Kilns,
Headington Quarry,
Oxford

8 Sept[ember] 1962

Dear Denise

I am delighted to hear that you liked the Narnian books, and it was nice of you to write and tell me. There *is* a map at the end of some of them in some editions.[65] But why not do one yourself! And why not write stories for yourself to fill up the gaps in Narnian history? I've left you plenty of hints—especially where Lucy and the Unicorn are talking in *The Last Battle*. I feel *I* have done all I can!

All good wishes,

Yours
C. S. Lewis

[65]Maps appeared only in the British editions of four of the Narnian books as follows: *Prince Caspian* ("A Map of Narnia and Adjoining Lands"—including part of the Wild Lands of the North and Archenland to the south); *The Voyage of the "Dawn Treader"* ("A Map of the First Part of the Voyage"—including the Seven Isles, the Lone Islands, and the Great Eastern Ocean); *The Silver Chair* ("A Map of the Wild Lands of the North"); *The Horse and His Boy* ("A Map of Archenland and the Desert"). All of these maps are pen and ink drawings by Pauline Baynes.

30 Nov[ember 19]62

Dear [Kathy]
    Thanks for your very kind letter and greetings. I was 64 yesterday. I am so glad you like my books.
    With all good wishes.

Yours sincerely
C. S. Lewis

❖

The Kilns, Kiln Lane,
Headington Quarry,
Oxford.
29th December 1962.

Dear Joan,
    Time? Wait till you reach my age and you will find that time doesn't go "fast" but at space speed! I see from my index that we have been corresponding since 1954 however, which is quite a respectable time, isn't it? Attached to your card is a photo of yourself in those days, and no doubt you look very different now. You have one consolation which I have not; for you, from now onwards and for many years, times will get better and better.
    How exciting to be both an opera singer and a cellist. And what a gift it will be for your Press Agent—"It is not commonly known that Miss Joan . . ., the world-famous opera singer, could have been a brilliant success in quite another section of the entertainment world. . . ."

I shudder at the subjects you have to take in High School, and some of them I could not even begin to attempt—Algebra and Calculus for example. I don't know anything about the University of Toronto, but have heard that it is good; I should however have thought you could have found what you wanted nearer home.

Every place seems to have had a severe cold wave this winter. I saw in the paper yesterday that there is skiing in Barcelona and snow on the peach blossom in Sicily. Looks as if one would have to go down to the latitude of Brazil or thereabouts to get warm. All the same, I'm astonished at conditions in Florida, where I thought it was always mild. Here we are having our hardest winter for fourteen years, and it is doing my old bones a bit of no good.

With all hopes for your success, and best wishes for 1963,

> yours sincerely,
> C. S. Lewis

❖

> The Kilns,
> Headington Quarry,
> Oxford

26 March [19]63

Dear Hugh
    . . . Don't get any more girls to write to me, though, unless they really need any help I might be

able to give. I have too many letters already. Remember me to the family.

yours
C. S. Lewis

❖

The Kilns,
Headington Quarry,
Oxford

26 March [19]63

Dear [Patricia]

Your letter was cheering, for *Till We Have Faces* has attracted less attention than any book I ever wrote. The names are just "made up". I expect some Jungianisms do come in but the main conscious prosework is Christian, not Jungian. Divine Love gradually conquers, first, a Pagan (and almost savage) soul's misconception of the Divine (as Ungit), then, shallow "enlightenment" (the Fox), and, most of all, her *jealousy* of the real God, whom she hates till near the end because she wants Psyche to be entirely hers.

yours sincerely,
C. S. Lewis

The Kilns,
Headington Quarry,
Oxford

27 March [19]63

Dear Joan

I see you've grown into a pretty woman. It must be a nice thing to be. The first poem is too rhapsodical—too much in the Whitman[66] tradition—for me, but then I'm a square. The best are "Do I the weak" and "And all is fair." So you are, like me, in love with syllables? Good. *Sheldar* is a pass-word. So are Tolkien's *Tinuviel* and *Silmaril*.[67] And David Lindsay's *Tormance* (in *Voyage to Arcturas*).[68] And *Northumberland* is glorious; but best of all, if only it meant something more interesting, is *silver salver*.

Nietzsche was a better poet than a philosopher. I give Plato better marks on both papers.

All the best,

Yours
C. S. Lewis

[66]Walt Whitman (1819–1892), American poet.

[67]From J. R. R. Tolkien's fantasy, *The Silmarillion*, which Lewis read in manuscript form although it was not published until 1977.

[68]*Voyage to Arcturus*, a fantasy novel by David Lindsay (1876–1945), which Lewis credited as the "father" of his own space trilogy.

23 April [19]63

Dear Kathy

Congratulations on keeping house!

By the way I also w[oul]d. say "I got a book". But your teacher and I are not "English teachers" in the same sense. She has to put across an idea of what the English language ought to be: I'm concerned entirely with what it *is* and however it came to be what it is. In fact she is a gardener distinguishing "flowers" from "weeds"; I am a botanist and am interested in both as vegetable organisms.

All good wishes,

Yours
C. S. Lewis

❖

The Kilns,
Headington Quarry
Oxford

11 July [19]63

Dear Joan

You *are* having a time! I think the poetry is developing alright. You'll be enchanted with imaginary names for a bit and probably go too far, but that will do you no harm. Like having had measles. I don't think Joyce[69] is as good at them as David Lindsay (*Voyage to Arcturus*) or E. R. Eddison in *The Worm*

---

[69]James Joyce (1882–1941), Irish novelist and poet.

Ouroboros.[70] His *silvamoonlake* is spoiled for me by the spelling which links it up with an advertisement slogan that we're all sick of here "Drinkapintamilkaday." For spelling counts as well as sound. I was astonished when someone first showed that by writing "cellar door" as *Selladore* one produces an enchanting proper name. Conversely, I can't enjoy *velvet* as a sound, lovely though it is, because I hate the stuff.

Zoroastrianism is one of the finest of the Pagan religions. Do you depend entirely on Nietzsche for your idea of it? I expect you w[oul]d. find it well worth time to look at the old sources.

Thanks for the photo. I hoped you were the centre one, it w[oul]d. have been horrid if you were Morna Glaney.

I'd write a better letter if I had not got a splitting headache.

Yours
C. S. Lewis

❖

The Kilns

7 Sept[ember 19]63

Dear Joan

Your letter is full of things that I'd like to reply to properly, but I'm not up to it. Last July I was thought to be dying. I am now an invalid, retired from all my

---

[70]*The Worm Ouroboros*, a fantasy by Eric Rucken Eddison (1882–1945).

job, and not allowed upstairs. My brother is away and I have to cope with all the mail. Forgive me,

Yours
C. S. Lewis

❖

[These last four letters were written less than a month before C. S. Lewis died on November 22, 1963. Each letter was typed, and no doubt composed with considerable assistance from Warren Lewis.]

The Kilns, Kiln Lane,
Headington Quarry,
Oxford.
26th October 1963.

Dear Ruth . . . ,

Many thanks for your kind letter, and it was very good of you to write and tell me that you like my books; and what a very good letter you write for your age!

If you continue to love Jesus, nothing much can go wrong with you, and I hope you may always do so. I'm so thankful that you realized [the] "hidden story" in the Narnian books. It is odd, children nearly *always* do, grown-ups hardly ever.

I'm afraid the Narnian series has come to an end, and am sorry to tell you that you can expect no more.

God bless you.

yours sincerely,
C. S. Lewis

The Kilns, Kiln Lane,
Headington Quarry,
Oxford.
29th October 1963.

Dear [Kathy],

Many thanks for your kind letter of the 23rd, and I'm sorry that the one you wrote me in the summer miscarried. How am I? I'm pretty well for a man who has become a permanent invalid, and if I cannot make much use of my legs I can still use my head, and am able to continue to write.

I hope you are enjoying your work on the newspaper, and that the savings programme will continue; there is no holiday so good as the one you have to save up for.

With all good wishes,

yours sincerely,
C. S. Lewis

The Kilns, Kiln Lane,
Headington Quarry,
Oxford.
11th November 1963.

Dear [Kathy],

Thanks for your note of the 5th, and I hope you will enjoy the *Screwtape Letters*[71] which has been the most popular of all my books.

I sympathize with your "maddening experience", but I can assure you that this is one of the occupational risks of authorship; the same sort of thing has happened to me more than once. There is nothing to be done about it!

With all best wishes,

yours sincerely,
C. S. Lewis

❖

The Kilns, Kiln Lane,
Headington Quarry,
Oxford.
21st November 1963.

Dear Philip . . . ,

To begin with, may I congratulate you on writing such a remarkably good letter; I certainly could not have written it at your age. And to go on with, thank you for telling me that you like my books, a thing an

---

[71]*The Screwtape Letters* (1942), fictional letters from an elderly devil in hell to a subordinate on earth.

author is always pleased to hear. It is a funny thing that all the children who have written to me see at once who Aslan is, and grown ups *never* do!

I haven't myself read the Puffin reprint you refer to, so of course missed the fault; but I will call the publisher's attention to it.

Please tell your father and mother [how] glad I am to hear that they find my serious books of some value.

With all best wishes to you and to them,

yours sincerely,
C. S. Lewis

[On Friday November 22, 1963, the day after this letter was typed, C. S. Lewis died peacefully at his home, The Kilns. His sixty-fifth birthday would have been the following week.]

An Annotated Children's Bibliography to C. S. Lewis

BOOKS:

The Chronicles of Narnia (listed in the order in which Lewis preferred that they be read—see Lewis's letter of April 23, 1957, to Laurence):

Lewis, C. S. *The Magician's Nephew*. Illustrations by Pauline Baynes. London: The Bodley Head, 1955; New York: The Macmillan Company, 1955.

    Explains the creation of Narnia and brings into the Chronicles two children named Digory and Polly. Their adventures with magic rings, a bad magician, and the evil Queen Jadis introduce them to the great lion, Aslan.

Lewis, C. S. *The Lion, the Witch and the Wardrobe*. Illustrations by Pauline Baynes. London: Geoffrey Bles, 1950; New York: The Macmillan Company, 1950. DELUXE EDITION: Illustrations by Michael Hague. New York: Macmillan Publishing Company, 1983.

    Introduces Peter, Edmund, Lucy, and Susan Pevensie to Aslan, the regal lion, who frees Narnia from the spell of the wicked White Witch.

Lewis, C. S. *The Horse and His Boy*. Illustrations by Pauline Baynes. London: Geoffrey Bles, 1954; New York: The Macmillan Company, 1954.

    Unfolds the story of how Bree, a Talking Horse, and Shasta, a young boy, escape from bondage. In the end they help Aslan and the Pevensie children save Narnia from foreign invasion.

Lewis, C. S. *Prince Caspian*. Illustrations by Pauline Baynes. London: Geoffrey Bles, 1951; New York: The Macmillan Company, 1951.

Relates how the four Pevensie children made a second
trip to Narnia where they find the land controlled by evil
Telmarines. The children, Prince Caspian, and an army of
Talking Beasts—with Aslan's help—conquer their enemies.

Lewis, C. S. *The Voyage of the "Dawn Treader."* Illustrations by
Pauline Baynes. London: Geoffrey Bles, 1952; New York:
The Macmillan Company, 1952.

Takes Lucy, Edmund, and their cousin, Eustace, on an
adventure aboard King Caspian's ship. By the time the ship
reaches the End of the World, the selfish and skeptical
Eustace is a follower of Aslan.

Lewis, C. S. *The Silver Chair*. Illustrations by Pauline Baynes.
London: Geoffrey Bles, 1953; New York: The Macmillan
Company, 1953.

Tells the story of Eustace and Jill's exciting mission. At
the request of Aslan, they set out to find and free Prince
Rilian, who is imprisoned by the Emerald Witch.

Lewis, C. S. *The Last Battle*. Illustrations by Pauline Baynes.
London: The Bodley Head, 1956; New York: The Macmillan
Company, 1956.

Reveals the final battle between the forces of evil and
Aslan's loyal followers. All of the characters (except Susan)
from the earlier stories rally together. Inspired by Aslan,
they fight the enemy and finally enter paradise.

Arnott, Anne. *The Secret Country of C. S. Lewis*. Grand Rapids,
Michigan: William B. Eerdmans Publishing Company,
1975.

A young people's biography of C. S. Lewis.

Gilbert, Douglas and Kilby, Clyde S. *C. S. Lewis: Images of His
World*. Grand Rapids, Michigan: William B. Eerdmans Publishing Company, 1973.

A photographic record of the people and places in
C. S. Lewis's life, including photographs of Lewis and his
family.

CALENDARS:

(The calendars include full-color original illustrations for each
month, as well as a full-length centerfold and cover piece.
The 1982, 1983, and 1984 calendars are out of print, but the
artwork for the 1982 calendar is reproduced in the Deluxe

Edition of *The Lion, the Witch and the Wardrobe*, illustrated by Michael Hague [New York: Macmillan Publishing Company, 1983]):

C. S. Lewis: *The Chronicles of Narnia 1982 Calendar. Book I: The Lion, the Witch and the Wardrobe*. Illustrated by Michael Hague. Macmillan Publishing Company.

C. S. Lewis: *The Chronicles of Narnia 1983 Calendar. Book II: Prince Caspian*. Illustrated by Michael Hague. Macmillan Publishing Company.

C. S. Lewis: *The Chronicles of Narnia 1984 Calendar. Book III: The Voyage of the "Dawn Treader."* Illustrated by Michael Hague. Macmillan Publishing Company.

FILM RENTAL:

C. S. Lewis: *The Lion, the Witch and the Wardrobe*. (Two reels—55 minutes each, or four reels—25 minutes each). Produced by Bob O'Donnell, Lord and King Associates.

Animated film may be rented from The Episcopal Radio-TV Foundation, 3379 Peachtree Road, N.E., Atlanta, Georgia 30326. Film was originally shown on CBS-TV. Rental includes study guide, *Aslan on the Move.*

NARNIA MAP:

A Map of Narnia and the surrounding countries. Created by Pauline Baynes. Based on the maps and writings of C. S. Lewis. New York: Macmillan Publishing Company, 1972.

A full-color poster map of Narnia with characters from each of the seven Chronicles.

PHOTOGRAPH OF THE WARDROBE:

A black and white photograph of the oak wardrobe that C. S. Lewis's brother, Warren, said was the inspiration for the wardrobe in the first of the Narnian books, *The Lion, the Witch and the Wardrobe*, is available from the Marion E. Wade Collection.

The wood in this wardrobe was adzed, assembled, and hand-carved by Lewis's grandfather, and stood for many years in his boyhood home of Little Lea, Belfast, Northern Ireland. It was later taken to stand in the hallway of his home, The Kilns, just outside Oxford.

For further information, please write the Marion E. Wade Collection, Wheaton College, Wheaton, Illinois 60187.

SOUND RECORDINGS:

(All of the following recordings are available both in cassette and record format; the stories are abridged):

Lewis, C. S. *The Magician's Nephew*. Read by Claire Bloom. Caedmon, 1995 Broadway, New York, N.Y. 10023.

Lewis, C. S. *The Lion, the Witch and the Wardrobe*. Read by Ian Richardson. Caedmon, 1995 Broadway, New York, N.Y. 10023.

Lewis, C. S. *The Horse and His Boy*. Read by Anthony Quayle. Caedmon, 1995 Broadway, New York, N.Y. 10023.

Lewis, C. S. *Prince Caspian*. Read by Claire Bloom. Caedmon, 1995 Broadway, New York, N.Y. 10023.

Lewis, C. S. *The Voyage of the "Dawn Treader."* Read by Anthony Quayle. Caedmon, 1995 Broadway, New York, N.Y. 10023.

Lewis, C. S. *The Silver Chair*. Read by Ian Richardson. Caedmon, 1995 Broadway, New York, N.Y. 10023.

Lewis, C. S. *The Last Battle*. Read by Michael York. Caedmon, 1995 Broadway, New York, N.Y. 10023.

ADDITIONAL MATERIALS FOR THE ADVANCED READER, PARENT, OR TEACHER

BOOKS:

Carpenter, Humphrey. *The Inklings: C. S. Lewis, J. R. R. Tolkien, Charles Williams, and Their Friends*. Boston: Houghton Mifflin Company, 1979.

A biographical study of the Inklings, friends of C. S. Lewis who shared a common interest in good conversation and literature.

Dorsett, Lyle W. *And God Came In: The Extraordinary Story of Joy Davidman, Her Life and Marriage to C. S. Lewis*. New York: Macmillan Publishing Company, 1983; Ballantine Epiphany Books, 1984.

Biography of C. S. Lewis's wife, Joy Davidman Gresham Lewis, including material on Lewis's stepsons,

David and Douglas Gresham. Photographs of Joy and C. S. Lewis.

Ford, Paul F. *Companion to Narnia*. San Francisco: Harper & Row, 1980.

A reader's guide in dictionary format to the themes, characters, and events in Narnia.

Green, Roger Lancelyn, and Hooper, Walter. *C. S. Lewis: A Biography*. New York: Harcourt Brace Jovanovich, 1974.

This is a full-scale biography

Hooper, Walter. *Past Watchful Dragons: The Narnian Chronicles of C. S. Lewis*. New York: Collier Books/Macmillan Publishing Co., 1979.

Information on the writing of Narnia.

Kilby, Clyde S., and Mead, Marjorie Lamp, eds. *Brothers and Friends: The Diaries of Major Warren Hamilton Lewis*. San Francisco: Harper & Row, 1982.

The diaries of C. S. Lewis's older brother, which contain material on Lewis's family and childhood and later life. Lewis family photographs.

Kilby, Clyde S. *The Christian World of C. S. Lewis*. Grand Rapids, Michigan: William B. Eerdmans Publishing Company, 1964.

General introduction to the thought and literary work of C. S. Lewis.

Lewis, C. S. *The Lion, the Witch and the Wardrobe*. STUDY EDITION. New York: Macmillan Publishing Company, 1979. Distributed by The Episcopal Radio-TV Foundation, Inc., Atlanta, Georgia.

This study guide (which includes the full text of the story) was prepared by The Right Reverend Harold Barrett Robinson and The Reverend Patricia Cadwallader. Includes study curriculum on three levels: children, early teens, adults.

Lewis, C. S. *On Stories and Other Essays on Literature*. Edited by Walter Hooper. New York: Harcourt Brace Jovanovich, 1982.

Lewis's thoughts on story, creativity, and writing.

Lewis, C. S. *Surprised by Joy: The Shape of My Early Life*. London: Geoffrey Bles, 1956; New York: Harcourt, Brace & World, 1956.

Lewis's autobiography including his childhood.

Sammons, Martha C. *A Guide through Narnia*. Wheaton, Illinois: Harold Shaw Publishers, 1979.

    Introduction to the Chronicles of Narnia, including an index of names and places, and a map and chronology.

Schakel, Peter J. *Reading with the Heart: The Way into Narnia*. Grand Rapids, Michigan: William B. Eerdmans Publishing Company, 1979.

    A literary introduction to the Chronicles of Narnia.

SOUND RECORDINGS:

(Available only in cassette):

Lewis, C. S. *Four Talks on Love*. Catacomb Cassettes, The Episcopal Radio-TV Foundation, 3379 Peachtree Road, N.E., Atlanta, Georgia 30326.

    Lewis reading from his own manuscript of *The Four Loves* (London: Geoffrey Bles, 1960; New York: Harcourt, Brace & World, 1960).

My dear Sarah — Please excuse me for not writing to you before to wish you a merry Christmas and a happy New Year and to thank you for your nice Card which I liked very much; I think you have improved in drawing cats and these were very good, much better than I can do. I can only draw a cat from the back view like this . I think it is rather cheating, don't you? because it does not show the face which is the difficult part to do. It is a funny thing that faces of people are easier to do then

most animals' faces except perhaps elephants and owls . I wonder why that should be! The reason I have not written before is that we have had a dreadfully busy time with people being ill in the house and visitors and pipes getting frozen in the frost. All the same I liked the frost (did you?); the woods looked really lovely with all the white on the trees, just like a picture to a story. But perhaps you were in London. I suppose it was not so nice there. We now have a Baby, about 6 weeks old, living in the house. It is a very quiet one and does not keep any of us

Insights,
Interviews
& More ...

Meet **Kaye Gibbons**

In 1997, Gibbons was awarded knighthood from the French Minister of Culture for her contributions to French literature. In 2001, she spoke at the Pompidou Center in Paris in what one journalist called, "an act of sustained brilliance." She has read and lectured to sold-out audiences from New York to Seattle. With domestic sales of more than 4.2 million copies and numerous worldwide translations, she was designated "one of the most lyrical writers working today" by *Entertainment Weekly* and described by one columnist as "a genius-Madonna in a black leather jacket," and by another as "a brilliant woman with old-fashioned star quality, rare."

Kaye Gibbons was born in 1960 in Nash County, North Carolina, on Bend of the River Road. She attended North Carolina State University and the University of North Carolina at Chapel Hill, studying American and English literature. At twenty-six, she wrote her first novel, *Ellen Foster*. Praised as an extraordinary debut, Eudora Welty said that "the honesty of thought and eye and feeling and word" mark the work of this talented writer, and Walker Percy said, "*Ellen Foster* is a Southern Holden Caulfield, tougher perhaps, as funny. A breathtaking first novel."

Ellen Foster was recently honored in London as one of the Twenty Greatest Novels of the Twentieth Century. In 1987, the novel won the Sue Kaufman Prize for first fiction from the American Academy and Institute of Arts and Letters, a Special Citation from the Ernest Hemingway Foundation, the Louis D. Rubin Writing Award, and numerous other major awards. Now a classic, it is taught in high schools and universities, often teamed with *The Adventures of Huckleberry Finn, The Catcher in the Rye,* and *To Kill a Mockingbird.* The book has been widely translated, frequently performed in theaters throughout the United States, and produced by Hallmark Hall of Fame as a TV-movie for CBS, starring Julie Harris and Jena Malone.

Published in 1989, *A Virtuous Woman* also received wide praise in the United States and abroad. The *San Francisco Chronicle* called the work "a perfect gem of a novel." Both *Ellen Foster* and *A Virtuous Woman* were chosen together as Oprah's Book Club selections in 1998, leading the *New York Times* bestseller list for many weeks.

In 1989, Gibbons received a grant from the National Endowment for the Arts to write a third novel, *A Cure for Dreams,* which was published in 1991. This novel won the 1990 PEN/Revson Award for the best work of fiction published by an American writer under thirty-five years of age, as well as the Heartland Prize for fiction from the *Chicago Tribune,* and other awards. In the novel she used transcripts from the Federal Writers' Project of the Great Depression. For the first time, she said, she "discovered the voice of ordinary men and women as a pure form of art and force of nature" and realized those voices would carry her through every novel she writes.

When *Charms for the Easy Life* was published in 1993, it became a *New York Times* bestseller and prompted a *Time* magazine reviewer to say, "Some people might give up their second born to write as well as Kaye Gibbons." This novel, which takes place between 1910 and 1945, in the home of three generations of highly intelligent and forthright women, ▶

Marion Ettlinger

Kaye Gibbons

" Some people might give up their second born to write as well as Kaye Gibbons. "

was filmed by Showtime Productions, and aired in October 2001, starring Mimi Rogers and Gena Rowlands. *Sights Unseen* (1995) was also a national bestseller and winner of the Critics Choice Award from the *San Francisco Chronicle*.

The following year, G. P. Putnam's Sons published her sixth novel, *On the Occasion of My Last Afternoon,* "a book of saints, sinners, and sorrows offering much pleasure," as one reviewer said. Readers agreed that it is "another cause for accolades" and many regarded it as her most brilliant to date.

Most recently, she was invited to become a member of the Fellowship of Southern Writers, a highly significant honor. She has received the Oklahoma Homecoming Award and was made a member of the YWCA Academy of Women. She was also chosen to write the introduction to the 2000 Modern Library Edition of Kate Chopin's *Awakening and Other Stories*.

Currently, she is working on journalistic pieces for publication and collection, a biography, and the sequel to *Ellen Foster*.

Gibbons lives in Raleigh, North Carolina, with her three daughters, Mary, nineteen; Leslie, sixteen; and Louise, fifteen. Her latest novel, *Divining Women,* is set during the 1918 influenza epidemic and was published by Putnam in April 2004. ᴄ⌒

A Discussion with
Kaye Gibbons

KAYE GIBBONS *recently summed up her philosophy of success when asked whether she was surprised by everything she has achieved thus far in her career.*

"I would've been surprised had I stumbled blindly into any of it, scratched a lottery ticket and found a prize that would then take me through the rest of my life. I wasn't 'lucky' that the books sold. I wasn't 'surprised' to learn that they're also taught in literature classes. That sounds arrogant, but it's not. To be able to write literature that sells takes an almost surreal amount of stubborn persistence; imagination; the ability to forego distractions, such as vacations, men, and alcohol; and a willingness to lock oneself in a room and submit oneself to constant, ruthless self-criticism. If a writer is any good, he or she will criticize himself so unmercifully that the reader and the reviewer either have to be misguided or wrong to make too much of a complaint. And there's something almost fun about fixing that deal in place. That sounds arrogant, and it may be. But it'd be more arrogant to subject readers, nice, hopeful people, to two hundred and fifty pages of words I had not tried to perfect, that I'd merely typed, as Hemingway said of meaningless writing. I know when it's being done to me, when clichés are bound or filmed and sold, and I don't appreciate it, the disrespect for this gift of language and for the people we're offering it to.

"But getting there, to that lucky, sacrificial place, requires long, long stretches of ▶

> " I wasn't 'surprised' to learn that [my books are] also taught in literature classes. That sounds arrogant, but it's not. "

A Discussion with Kaye Gibbons *(continued)*

unbroken concentration and more Diet Cokes than most people can or want to tolerate. I love the labor, the sheer manual labor that goes into making these books seem as though they were effortlessly written. I love what has come to feel like a habit of invention. I go about my days stunned that I didn't waste what Walker Percy called a 'knack' for writing.

"And there's the grace that comes when I'm in my daughters' presence. I go about stunned that I didn't drop or misplace my children or cause them to be expelled from school for repeating what they learned at home. You see, I live alone with three smart and sober teenage girls—it has taken skill, patience, stamina, and that same kind of 'knack'. And like this forty-year custom of reading and writing, the girls are a seriously profound, sustained joy.

"You see, I love what I do. I raise three human beings, and I do language for a living—it's only as terrifying as it is lovely." ❧

> ❝ I love the labor, the sheer manual labor that goes into making these books seem as though they were effortlessly written. ❞

A Timeline of the Key Dates of the Civil War

The *San Francisco Chronicle* wrote, "[*On the Occasion of My Last Afternoon*] is, above all, a story of how Southern women suffered and endured the deprivations of the home front during the Civil War ... and an unflinching literary indictment of the prideful landowners, politicians, and generals who gave birth to the War Between the States." Many people, events, and places made up the drama that was the four years of the Civil War. Take a close look at the timeline below to understand how these events unfolded.

November 6, 1860: Abraham Lincoln elected president of the United States.

December 20, 1860: South Carolina secedes from the Union.

December–April 1860: Mississippi, Florida, Alabama, Georgia, Louisiana, and Texas secede from the Union.

February 9, 1861: The Confederate States of America formed. Jefferson Davis named President.

March 4, 1861: Abraham Lincoln sworn in as President.

April 12, 1861: Fort Sumter in Charleston, South Carolina, is attacked and captured by the Confederates. The Civil War officially begins. ▶

66 An unflinching literary indictment of the prideful landowners, politicians, and generals who gave birth to the War Between the States. 99

7

The Facts Behind the Fiction (*continued*)

April 17, 1861: Virginia secedes from the Union, followed within five weeks by Arkansas, Tennessee, and North Carolina.

July 20, 1861: The Battle of Bull Run. The Union Army defeated.

February 6, 1862: Union General Ulysses S. Grant captures Fort Henry in Tennessee.

March 1862: The Peninsular Campaign begins. McClellan's Union Army of the Potomac marches towards Richmond.

April 6–7, 1862: 13,000 Union troops and 10,000 Confederates killed or wounded at the Battle of Shiloh in Tennessee.

April 24, 1862: New Orleans captured by the Union.

August 29–30, 1862: The Second Battle of Bull Run in Northern Virginia. The Union Army is defeated and retreats to Washington.

September 17, 1862: The Battle of Antietam in Maryland. The Confederates under Lee are defeated and 26,000 men die.

September 22, 1862: President Lincoln issues the Emancipation Proclamation, freeing the slaves.

December 13, 1862: Union troops defeated at Fredericksburg, Virginia.

May 1–4, 1863: The Union Army defeated by Confederates at Chancellorsville.

66 President Lincoln issues the Emancipation Proclamation, freeing the slaves. 99

May 10, 1863: Confederate General Stonewall Jackson dies from wounds inflicted during battle.

July 1–3, 1863: The Confederates defeated at the Battle of Gettysburg in Pennsylvania. The war changes course as the South loses ground.

July 4, 1863: Confederates defeated at the Battle of Vicksburg. The Union takes control of the Mississippi River, splitting the Confederacy in two.

September 19–20, 1863: The Confederates beat the Union troops in a decisive victory at Chickamauga, Georgia.

November 19, 1863: The Gettysburg Address.

November 23–25, 1863: Union troops, trapped in Chattanooga, Tennessee, are besieged by the Confederate Army. The Union troops prevail.

May 4, 1864: Grant's massive army of 120,000 begins its march towards Richmond and Lee's Army of Northern Virginia.

July 20, 1864: The Battle of Atlanta begins.

September 2, 1864: General Sherman officially captures Atlanta.

November 15, 1864: Sherman begins his march to the sea, capturing Savannah, Georgia, on **December 21, 1864**.

April 9, 1865: Robert E. Lee surrenders to Ulysses S. Grant at Appomattox Courthouse in Virginia.

April 14, 1865: President Lincoln shot. He dies the next day.

> *Confederates defeated at the Battle of Vicksburg. The Union takes control of the Mississippi River, splitting the Confederacy in two.*

A Reading Excerpt
Divining Women

Autumn 1918: Rumors of peace are spreading across America, but spreading even faster are the first cases of Spanish influenza, whispering of the epidemic to come. Maureen Ross, well past a safe childbearing age, is experiencing a difficult pregnancy. Her husband, Troop—cold and careless of her condition—is an emotional cripple who has battered her spirit throughout their marriage. As Maureen's time grows near, she becomes convinced she will die in childbirth. Into this loveless ménage arrives Mary Oliver, Troop's niece. The sheltered child of a well-to-do, freethinking Washington family, Mary comes to help Maureen in the last weeks of her confinement, and through their time together, ultimately helps her find strength and spiritual renewal.

Read on for a look at the book that the San Antonio Express-News *calls "the most powerful writing yet from Gibbons."*

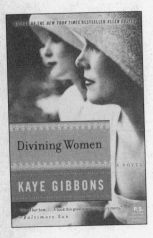

I GREW UP around three women who did not ask permission before they offered me a view of their wide and deep universe, and even now, at forty-three, I still find that much of my outlook comes from a continuously looping reel of memories, and I am able to see and hear what they felt, thought, and did. When I have fallen, it has invariably been through the places they left for me to discover for myself. And when I have luxuriated in any reward of love or labor, even if I have every right to claim the accomplishment for myself, when enough layers of time are peeled away, there is always a scene of a lesson being taught, sometimes taken, sometimes not. But there is always a correspondence between the lesson and the reward.

My mother must have worked on my lesson plans the whole trip back from North Carolina, after Nora's funeral, although my grandmother's required no preparation. Because of the concerns that arose after Mother brought the news that my uncle was marrying a person who appeared stable and pulled together, with no obvious history as a mental patient, the three of them seemed to swivel around and see me, at fifteen, as suddenly vulnerable and in danger of being fooled, manipulated, and then abandoned by a man. Even from hundreds of miles away, they had decided that Maureen and Troop's incongruous match amounted to nothing more than the promise of misery for her and the threat of something similar for me.

After Mother reported on her initial impression of Maureen, she exiled the men from the house, explaining that the company of women was best for me now, but when they were gone she said, "The truth is that my father is too tenderhearted to hear what his son did to me. What happened when I was alone with Troop after the funeral is in a different category entirely from anything he and his mother have ever sent our way. And I also could not tell him how much Maureen reminded me of you, Mary. You and she have the same trusting look on your face that tells people that you're more than likely going to believe anything they say. There were small things as well, the way you both stand and look out over a room, the way fabric fits you in the hips. But mainly it was the way she tilted her head and smiled as I spoke—it made me feel anyone could spot that open nature and step right in to take advantage of her." ▶

> 66 Because of the concerns that arose after Mother brought the news that my uncle was marrying a person who appeared stable and pulled together, with no obvious history as a mental patient, the three of them seemed to swivel around and see me, at fifteen, as suddenly vulnerable and in danger of being fooled, manipulated, and then abandoned by a man. 99

Grandmother Louise said, "My theory is that she has some family money. Being from Mississippi, her father may own a plantation. Troop wants the slaves and the money."

Mother sighed and told her that plantations were merely large farms and did not require slaves to run them. "No, Maureen wasn't raised anywhere near any kind of money," she said. "Her family's poor."

When I told my mother how amazed I was that someone she'd just met would disclose something as awful as that, she replied, "No, she said nothing about it. Her fingernails did. They were ridged, furrowed, like garden rows." They knew, but I learned that this is an unmistakable indication of childhood malnourishment. Sadness for this stranger washed over me, and I needed to know more about her.

"Well," Mother said, "I said that she was tall. And she wore her clothes well on her body, which I know is an odd thing to say, but she did."

Grandmother Louise said, "What did she have on? Tell me. I'm interested. We can tell if she called this turmoil on herself."

Louise Canton Oliver was a tiny woman with lovely café-au-lait skin and such small hands and feet that she had to wear children's gloves and shoes. Her clothing had to be cut from little girls' patterns, but she would order only black fabrics, which absorbed heat and kept her pleasingly warm to the bone and also gave her the overall air of a deadly serious child. Although she had this unchanged and odd habit of dressing, she was the one who provided a running narration when we watched the ultra-ultra set parade at the

> 66 Her clothing had to be cut from little girls' patterns, but she would order only black fabrics, which absorbed heat and kept her pleasingly warm to the bone and also gave her the overall air of a deadly serious child. 99

Waldorf. The current designs and trends were all familiar to her, and she was able to speak of them with an uncanny facility. We knew that if mother could provide a thorough inventory of Maureen's clothing, my grandmother could give a fairly exacting analysis of her character and possibly even of why she was letting herself in for such trouble. It was my grandmother's chosen method of divination in a family that listened to the counsel of cards, fate boards, tea leaves, and ghosts, and I had long believed that she was far more reliable than these. Hers was that only authority that was left unquestioned, something that could not be said of the various temperamental prophets who were hired to give reading without first understanding that my family might debate and amend any unsuitable or inconvenient destinies. ∽

> 66 It was my grandmother's chosen method of divination in a family that listened to the counsel of cards, fate boards, tea leaves, and ghosts. 99

Have You **Read?**

Sights Unseen

The outside world can pose a serious challenge for children, and the family home should be a place that provides respite and safety. But in the days when serious mental illnesses were described in the crudest of terms and treated with the harshest of methods, young Hattie Barnes lives with a mother who is known around town as the "Barnes woman with all the problems." Hattie and her brother endure the complexities of living with a woman with very little aptitude for housework, family responsibilities, and—even more importantly—providing her children with the stability and support that they need.

In a lesser family, things could have disintegrated into chaos and despair. But Hattie is blessed with a loving and patient father who still deeply loves his beautiful but troubled wife and makes every effort to keep the family together through the turbulent ups and downs of what we would today recognize as her bipolar disorder. The wonderful Pearl, the family housekeeper, lends the children the portion of mothering they desperately need. And as Hattie looks back at a childhood that was peppered with shame, fear, and insecurity, she is able to see through the clouds and remember the bond that came from the many challenges—a bond that in the end made them all stronger.

PRAISE FOR *SIGHTS UNSEEN*

"Beautifully crafted and intense, Kaye Gibbons's novels are marked by an emotional authenticity that never falters."

—*People*

Charms for the Easy Life

In the verdant backwoods of North Carolina,
in a sad and singular era, the Birches are
unique among women of their time—living
gloriously rich if decidedly offbeat lives in a
private world abandoned by men. And though
misery often beats a path to their door,
headstrong Sophia and her shy, brilliant
daughter Margaret possess charms to ward
off loneliness and despair—thanks to the
uncompromising strength, uncommon
wisdom, and muscular love of a remarkable
matriarch and self-taught healer who calls
herself Charlie Kate.

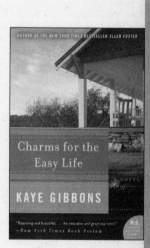

PRAISE FOR *CHARMS FOR THE EASY LIFE*

*"Haunting and beautiful . . . an evocative and
gracious novel."*

—*New York Times Book Review*

The Web Detective

*For more information or to sign up for
Kaye Gibbons's mailing list, please visit* `
www.kayegibbons.com

http://www.civilwar.com/
For more information on the Civil War

**http://www.civilwarhome.com/
civilwarnurses.htm**
*For information on the heroic role of nurses
during the Civil War*

**http://www.ah.dcr.state.nc.us/sections/
capitol/stat_cap/civwar.htm**
*For more information on Raleigh, North
Carolina, and its place in the Civil War*